Advance Praise for Buying Time

"*Buying Time* is a great guide for young people looking to learn more about personal development, financial growth, mental health and other principles entrepreneurs typically learn far too late in life. I wish I had this book when I was young."

—*Scott Duffy, founder of AI Mavericks*

"*Buying Time* is more than a great introduction to the subject of personal development. Complete with insights on financial hygiene I wish everyone knew, it is guaranteed to have a major impact on anyone who reads it."

—*Tony Child, founder of Elevated Worldwide*

"Offering real talk on getting out of debt, saving for the future and making your business thrive, Heidi's approach is all about keeping it real, focusing on what really matters and making a difference rather than just making money. For anyone looking to find their footing in a chaotic world, *Buying Time* is a must-read that makes the complexity of personal finance feel like a coffee chat."

—*Maresa Friedman, Fortune 100 Strategist, founder of Executive Cat Herder and the Strategy Solved newsletter*

BUYING TIME

A Young

Person's Guide

to Building

Wealth and

Fulfillment

HEIDI MCNULTY

LEGACY
launch pad
PUBLISHING

ISBN: 978-1-956955-94-1 (ebook)

ISBN: 978-1-956955-95-8 (paperback)

ISBN: 978-1-956955-96-5 (hardback)

Cover Design: onegraphica.com

For more information about Heidi or to get the accompanying workbook, please visit:

This book is dedicated to my children:
Kaden, Cole and Miles McNulty.

We have been through so much, and I am so proud of the young men you are becoming. I can only hope that I have done a good job at being an example of what you are capable of. I hope I taught you the lessons in this book by example and that you will lead fulfilling successful lives despite the trauma we've experienced. I love you guys, and I hope you know that you have been my motivation to do all things.

I promise to continue to grow each and every day to become my best self and be the best mom I can be.

Contents

Introduction

How do you define success?

Do you imagine properties around the world? Expansive compounds with stunning views? Do you picture yourself driving a Maserati along the California coast? Maybe you see yourself as a CEO, taking calls from a helicopter on your way to the Hamptons, flying over traffic and the people who work nine-to-five jobs, making money for people like you.

What about your personal life? Is it your dream to remain perpetually single? Or do you imagine a family—kids enrolled in elite schools, vacations on your yacht and generations of wealth in the bank?

Now the big question:

How will you get from where you are today to living the life of your wildest dreams?

How will you transform yourself from someone with car payments who pays rent to a landlord into that millionaire with a six-car garage and other people writing checks to you? How much time do you see passing? A decade? Twenty or 30 years? How old will you be when you retire?

When I first set out to write this book, I couldn't wait to teach young people how to become successful entrepreneurs and build wealth just like I did, leading to early retirement. It has always been my goal to help young people design the lives of their dreams, built on a solid foundation of financial security. I wanted to teach others about my experience grinding, saving money and building businesses, and that it was an accessible and achievable path to financial freedom and success that anyone could follow.

Coming from next-to-nothing, I mapped my own course when I was 19 (and if I can do it, anyone can!). At just 35 years old, I sold my business and decided to retire—I was ready to live out the rest of my life enjoying my family and the fruits of my labor. I couldn't wait to share my roadmap to wealth with others—but then, life hit me. Hard.

Roadmaps don't prepare you for collision, and there is no manual for navigating trauma when your spouse takes his life, leaving you a widow with three children. I retired early, but I was also a very young widow. Every bit of momentum I'd built into my life and career since I was a teenager came to an abrupt halt. Forced to look at the wreckage of this tragedy, I also had to deconstruct and rebuild everything I had achieved upon a new foundation—a brand new value system.

When tragedy struck, mindset work wasn't totally new to me. My husband had been struggling for years with PTSD and mental health problems, and I learned that I could only really help him if I began shifting my focus from setting and achieving professional goals to discovering the joy in the journey towards them. During this time, instead of channeling my energy into building wealth, I began to see the abundance in my life more clearly, and I wanted to appreciate all that I had and share that gratitude with others.

But it wasn't until the rug of life was pulled out from under me that I really understood that my big bank account could not be my sole source of gratitude. Life itself is enough. And as my values shifted again, I learned that a deeper well of gratitude is what leads us to *every* kind of abundance. My evolving financial philosophy and value system ultimately has allowed me to experience the benefits of looking at life through a lens of love, not lack.

In this book, I combine my winning business strategies with an abundance- and love-based mindset, helping you to buy yourself time to experience and enjoy the finest lifestyle while living generously and in the moment. I hope to share the evolution of my values, my mindset and the lessons I've learned through the various stages of my life—adolescence, young adulthood and where I am today: living in financial, mental and spiritual abundance as an early retiree in my 30s.

Through each chapter, I'll take you through the story of my life while outlining the lessons I learned and the wealth-building strategies I used that anyone can follow for similar results. (Please note that to dive even deeper into these lessons and for more prompts and forms you can fill out and use, *The Buying Time Workbook* is also available for purchase online on Amazon and other major bookselling platforms.)

As you embark on a life journey towards building success, I want you to already understand that real, unwavering success is a combination of financial and emotional security, so that no matter what comes your way, you are safe and secure enough to not only survive, but thrive—*no matter what happens*.

I am still just as passionate about helping young people to become experts at what they love, and how to turn that passion into profit. But instead of only teaching financial and budgeting strategies, I want to help you start your journey with purposeful planning and with a mindset of values-focused awareness. What is most important to you? How can you embody your values in your daily life and in your work? How will you define and find fulfillment?

My goals have evolved with time and experience. While they used to be solely career, money and financial success-oriented, today they are very different. Today, the way I create value in my daily life is by setting a daily intention to be inspiring, loving and generous. That is my new goal and my definition of success.

Now let's define your passion so you can use it as the key to unlock a future of financial freedom with an unshakable foundation of love and generosity.

Chapter One
BROKE AND BROKEN DOWN...AGAIN

There was a shooting at this mall—my mom and I saw it on the news later. My friends and siblings all knew already that the mall was unsafe; it was in a part of our northern California town that was commonly known as a "bad neighborhood." Though we didn't know the full context at the time, my mom and I were there when the shooting happened—because it was an active crime scene, we were stranded there and had been for quite some time.

The three-hour mark came and went, and all we could do was sit still, waiting. We had the windows of our 1980-something Hyundai rolled down despite the 103-degree heat because the air conditioner didn't work, and we were desperate for air. I couldn't relax, and my eyes were darting everywhere at any movement, looking out for signs of danger. I imagined what the five o'clock news would say about us: *This just in—a mother and her 12-year-old daughter fatally shot, sitting in their junky car just off the freeway, on their way to what everyone knows is a dangerous mall...*

It wasn't the first time I had been stranded in my family car in unsafe conditions. The last time Mom and I were on a California freeway during a traffic jam, again in 103-degree heat, we were on our way to dance class—just 10-year-old me in a leotard and tights, hair in a bun, shoes in my dance bag, staring out the rolled-down window in suffocating heat, praying for a breeze and for the cars ahead of us to move. Hours went by, and my dance class started and ended. Not only did I miss my dance class, I also got sick from sitting in that hot car for so long.

It's hard to say which was worse: the worry and unknowns I'd had as a confused and scared little kid who had to trust that the adults in my life had things handled, or this time, as a pre-teenager who knew about real danger and understood that help wasn't coming any time soon. We were stuck in a terrifying neighborhood, waiting for dad to finish work so he could come attempt to help us.

Why couldn't he just tell his boss there was a family emergency? It was hard not to think about our other car (the good car) just sitting there in his work parking lot while we sat suffocating and putting our lives at risk by a sketchy Macy's. It didn't seem fair that Dad drove the nice car to work and it just sat there all day while mom was forced to chauffeur me around in an unreliable junky car that was always breaking down. There was a theme in my life of feeling afraid because of financial insecurity.

Mom, Dad and Money

Mom and Dad were always bickering about money and expenses—how Mom managed the money, and Dad spent it. There was a lot of talk about credit cards. They each spent money differently and had dueling philosophies on how it should be managed. Dad spent it as he earned it—buying us kids whatever we wanted without really thinking about whether we could afford it or not. Mom was always playing catch up, robbing Peter to pay Paul, juggling credit card balances and drained checking accounts, paying off one card with another, always in a stress fever over the climbing balances that were never getting paid off.

Like a lot of traditional families, my dad worked and my mom managed the household: the chores, errands, kids, shopping and bill-paying. As an adult, I can see how both roles are equally stressful: one responsible for earning enough money for a family with five kids to live a comfortable life, and the other responsible for managing the chaos and keeping everyone happy.

I was the youngest, and my four older siblings all grew up in a completely different world from mine. They all grew up in Utah, where most families lived in modest homes and drove sensible cars. Every family was on a budget, and it was considered immoral and showy to brag about wealth or to show off with flashy cars and enormous homes.

From the time I was seven, my family lived in a suburb of Sacramento, California—a world away from the modesty of Utah. Cars, homes, neighborhoods and clothes were all opportunities to show off just how much you had. Name brands, the right zip code and foreign cars were just normal. In Utah, everyone was the Joneses. In California, there was always a richer Jones family on the next block.

I don't think my dad was necessarily trying to be someone he wasn't—he wanted to do well and to have nice things. Who doesn't? But dad was an instant-gratification kind of guy; if he wanted it, he bought it without thinking too much about the impact on the bank accounts. Mom would then do the intricate dance with credit cards and paychecks that didn't stretch far enough to cover the bills. He used the family credit cards for work expenses, but was then forgetful about submitting his expense reports on time, so when his company got around to reimburse him, the due date for the AMEX bill had come and gone. I remember my mom crying at the kitchen table, surrounded by letters demanding money, forcing her to take out loans to cover bills. Those loans to cover the overdue bills caused even more stress. There was a time I cried to my teacher because all I wanted was to go with my friends to get something to eat after school, but we didn't have any money. There was never enough, but we were always spending.

The emotional weight from money stress meant we were always walking on eggshells when it came to money. We always had everything we needed, but the paychecks didn't last from one to the next. We had a nice house, each with our own bedroom, in a nice enough neighborhood, and in general, my parents didn't say "no" when we asked for something, even though they couldn't really afford to say "yes"—it went on the credit card. Our family didn't have healthy spending habits or communication about budgets and money. We actually didn't talk about it at all, and when my parents did communicate, it was usually a stressful argument. But this also meant that my mom and I found ourselves stranded in broken down cars. And what I remember more than the heat, the beads of sweat rolling down the backs of my legs or my mom silently swallowing her stress and resentment was how I felt: Afraid. Unsafe. Insecure.

Family Values Versus Money Values

As I got older and would compare what my friends had to how and where we lived, it always felt like even though we appeared to have what other families had, they enjoyed something we never seemed to have: stability. I didn't have the word for it then, but now I know that what I longed for was security. I didn't want to feel unsafe or in danger of losing everything.

It's very normal for our family of origin and our learned attitudes about money to play a major role in how we look at money as we grow up and develop habits. A lot of the time, we are reacting to those original ideas. While I want to support you as you create wealth and financial security, I want you to do it from a place of security, not fear. It's going to take some deep diving and some work on your part, but I promise it will be worth it. Regardless of where or who you come from, if you want a clear path towards success and don't have clarity about your past, that path will be longer—old habits and ideas will hold you back from making progress.

In those years, the early messaging I'd received about money and the fears that it instilled in me lit a fire that would burn for decades and helped me build everything I have today. Every kid has dreams about what they want to be when they grow up. My dreams were simple: I vowed to myself that I would never live in financial insecurity. I would never struggle to pay bills or fight about money. When I was in sixth grade, I made a decision that turned into a commitment I made to myself: one day, I would be rich. I would be a millionaire.

Chapter One Insight Exercises

Giving in to instant gratification means suffering in the big picture, and ultimately, more time in the workforce. All the little things you buy today are holding you back if they're not in line with your big-picture goals. This is everything from car payments to daily coffee to drinks with friends. The more you spend today on things you don't need, the more you have to work to earn money to replace that money, keeping you from that forward-moving momentum.

I learned quickly that if I wanted to build a foundation of wealth, I needed to delay gratification and save my money. My early years were very lean years. But it paid off and bought me time later on in life.

As we begin this journey together, here are some (maybe tough!) questions to get you started, so you can see how you evolve from one chapter to the next:

1. Make a "guess" list of all of your expenses. What do you estimate you spend on bills every month? What do you guess you spend on food and entertainment?
2. Now create a *real* budget worksheet (model yours off the example after these exercises—and please note that this form and others are available in *The Buying Time Workbook*).
3. Go through your bank statement and record every actual expense. Every single thing you see on your bank statement goes on the budget sheet.
4. Categorize each expense—utilities, household expenses, groceries, entertainment.
5. Where are you surprised by your expenses?
6. Now look at each line item and ask yourself, "Where can I save money?" For instance, if your cable bill is $120, what if you canceled cable and purchased shows a la carte? Or what if you listened to free podcasts instead? You'd also be bettering yourself and expanding your knowledge base. If you're a sports fan, what if you watched games at a local bar instead? The cost of a beer or soda is cheaper than $120 per month. Remember that every little amount equates to a big number when you look at the big picture. You are committed to the big picture.

7. Based on the commitment to savings you've made above, what can you realistically put into savings each month? What do those monthly savings translate to over 12 months? Every increment adds up fast.

8. Set up a savings account and an automatic transfer of that amount from your main account every month. What other tripwires can you put in place that will help you keep that money out of sight and out of mind? For example, if you choose a small bank that is on the other side of town, it will become inconvenient to access those funds.

9. How can you delay gratification—what are some daily steps you can take to build up your savings?

10. What were the messages you learned about money in your family of origin? How do you feel when you think about money? How does it feel when you talk about money with someone else?

11. What are your money goals? Write your vision for this week, this month, this year, this decade and so forth.

12. Make a chart with two columns. On the left, write down all of the old ideas about money and success you have and that you want to let go of. Now on the right, write down how you *want* to feel about money and wealth.

13. Identify *one* obstacle that could potentially hold you back from achieving your life's goals and dreams, whether it's a feeling or a belief. Try to distill that down to one word (for me it was "fear"). Now write the *opposite* of that word (the opposite of fear is "faith" or "confidence").

14. Imagine the life of your dreams. What does it look like? When you look at your bank account in this fabulous future, how do you feel? How is it different from how you feel today?

15. Take that "future feeling" and make it your daily goal. You can use the law of attraction by going throughout your life today focused on those feelings and attracting more of that to you.

16. Now what is *one way* you can celebrate your success so far?

Sample Worksheets

The QR code at the beginning of this book will lead you to the *Buying Time Workbook*, which has some sample worksheets you can use to get a better picture of your financial standing at any given time.

Chapter Two
THE VALUE OF VALUES

B efore we begin this journey of life and wealth building together, we need to talk about values—the foundation of everything you are building. If you don't have clarity about what drives you, your boat will be rudderless and your car won't have an engine. Any success you achieve will be shallow and lacking depth and, well, value.

Values are principles. They are your ethics, morals and the belief system that determines what you consider most important in life. Values are often informed by how you were raised, but they aren't fixed. Sometimes we carry into adulthood those same values we were taught as children as ways to understand what is right and what is wrong. Common values include being respectful to others, placing family above all others and being honest, as well as how to behave in various situations. All of these things serve as a guide to help us make decisions in life.

The Impact of "Traditional" Values

Many people are raised with what some would call "traditional" values that are often based on a religious framework. If you think about the word "tradition," it implies that ideas, customs and beliefs are passed down from one generation to the next. From one religious philosophy to the next, traditions change, as will values. Many people are raised in communities where the majority of people around them share the same traditions—this is true all over the world.

Sometimes people are raised in complicated or stressful environments that lack structure and values, and it leaves them floundering as they move through life. Unless there is a disruptive experience—perhaps meeting and working with a religious leader, a community resource or a mentor—they may not even know that they are missing a stable foundation of guiding principles that help them navigate life. Unless they have an opportunity to really focus on themselves and decide what's important to them, even if they do succeed at some things in life, they may not be able to fully enjoy the benefits, and their success may be fleeting. Their relationships—personal and professional—may suffer.

Many of us go through transformative experiences that wind up changing us and our values in tandem. Perhaps we find a friend or mentor who inspires us to be the best version of ourselves no matter what is going on around us, whether we are rich or poor, healthy or sick. Some people end up traveling or moving away from the comfort of what they've always known, challenging what were previously fixed ideas—sometimes for generations. Seeing the world through new eyes helps them reshape their value system as they learn that there are many ways to live. You may believe something very different today than what you were raised to believe—developing your own set of values can be liberating and empowering! But whether we are carrying on with the same traditions and beliefs we were raised with or are starting from scratch, having a clear idea of what our values are will help us better understand where we come from and how to pave the path to where we want to go.

In my journey to becoming wealthy and healthy—inside and out—I realized that I had to surround myself with the best and brightest minds in both investing and mindset coaching.

I was lucky enough to find a world-renowned mentor, Dave Austin.

The World According to Dave Austin

Dave has had a fascinating life and career. He's been a successful Hollywood actor, received a *Presidential Merit Award* from the Grammys and is a published author with more than one million books sold. He has been a successful real estate developer, former corporate executive, has owned multiple independent record labels and is a retired professional athlete. He is an international speaker, having lectured in front of audiences everywhere from Harvard to the United Nations, and in countries as far away as India and Uzbekistan. His book, *Be A Beast: Unleash Your Animal Instincts for Performance Driven Results*, has cemented his position as a premiere mental performance and mindset coach, connecting him with Olympians, world-class athletes in the NFL, MLB, PGA and the ATP Tour, as well as working with the Pentagon, US Army Rangers, Navy SEALs and Fortune 500 companies—and even entrepreneurs like me. His unique approach involves a visualization technique that helps people maximize their talents and hone in on their own competitive edge.

I am honored to call him a friend, and he has allowed me to sift through his personal experience and expertise to include some gems and advice within this book, so be on the lookout for a few of Dave's tips!

With that said, I asked Dave as to what he learned about money at a young age and how those early ideas have changed over time. Here's what he said:

> *I would say around the age of eight or nine, I started to realize that my grandfather was extremely successful and financially well-to-do. He was executive vice president of Bell Telephone, one of the largest companies in the world at that time. My dad, on the other hand, was a Navy chaplain, and even though he held an important leadership role serving as a Navy Officer, it seemed my dad never had "enough" money. My mom was an only child, and coming from a wealthy family, I saw a bit of friction in terms of finances while growing up. My dad's attitude was, if there was a TV to buy, you bought the cheapest one—whereas my grandfather thought if there was a TV to buy, you had to buy the best one available. As a kid seeing these opposing mindsets, I think that probably shaped my worldview, and even though I tend to be more like my dad, I'm really more of a blend.*
>
> *For me, I never worried about money since we seemed to have enough and were okay. My dad had a good salary and a secure job. We weren't millionaires, but we were in a very secure place. Money was simply never anything I was concerned about.*
>
> *Then, when I was out on my own, money became a bigger issue for me—especially when I needed to provide for my own family, since I got married in college. Quickly, I had to provide for my wife and then for my*

*son. And I don't think I got this from my dad or my
mom, but I had this incredible feeling that I didn't want
to have too much money because, as I saw for some other
people, it was like the root of all evil. Most of the people
I knew that had a lot of money were jerks. My grandpar-
ents were the exception.*

*And so, I did my best not to hold onto too much money. I
had just enough to do this or that. Eventually, I kind of
woke up to the idea that it's okay to have money and that
I could be different and handle it better than how I
perceived others who had a lot of money doing it.*

*At one point, my wife, Cathy, talked me into attending
this big seminar hosted by a man named T. Harv Eker—
"The Millionaire Mind" was the name of this three-day
workshop, and I begrudgingly went. I didn't care about
that kind of stuff. I remember Harv asked, "Who are you,
money-wise?" From his perspective, he had us grouped
as the spenders, the savers, the avoiders and the spiritual
monks. Well, I went right to the monk section, even
though my wife thought I should go be with the avoiders.
I thought the "monks" most likely believed that money
was the root of all evil, and therefore lived with a holier-
than-thou mentality. That was a better fit for me.*

*I believe my wife went with the "spenders" corner of the
room, to the ones brave enough to know that you can
always make more money. To me, that would be where
the investors would go. The "savers" on the other hand,
are too nervous to risk loss. They just hold on to whatever they have, believing they can't make the "big
money." Us "monks" make sure we don't have too much*

money because, well, we're spiritual—but when you look closer at those who spend freely, you realize that money can be an abundant thing.

Values and Motivation

In addition to values, we all have motivating factors that steer us towards our goals. Some are born into generational wealth, and their goal is to maintain that wealth, so perhaps they are driven by a desire to keep their elders happy. Some are born into poverty, and their motivation is a deep desire to live differently, to achieve a level of success that lifts them and future generations out of financial insecurity.

For me, a big motivator from a young age was fear. I didn't want to live the way my parents did—worrying and bickering about money. Living paycheck to paycheck. Never knowing whether the rug would be pulled out from under us or the car would break down on the freeway.

When I had kids, I didn't want them to worry or suffer the way I did.

I think maybe because I couldn't control my financial environment growing up, I became very driven from a young age and adopted an "I'll show them" attitude that ultimately served me well! This mentality helped me build the foundation of all the success I have today. It drove me. I may have been driven by fear in those early years, but I was driven.

Very early on, I decided that having money leads to safety, reliability, security, freedom from worry, stress and arguments. In many ways, I still believe that to be true. If money is a tool, having a tool—or a whole bunch of tools!—to help with your problems sounded pretty great to me! But looking back, I wasn't really happy in those early years of independence and wealth building. I based my self-worth on how much I was making; my value was my net worth. I was so focused on my financial goals that I failed to incorporate any kind of emotional or joy-based goals. I was unbalanced. Because I was so intent to delay my gratification, I often felt suicidal on birthdays because I hadn't reached that "millionaire status" yet. Even if I had met one, some or many of my goals, I ultimately still felt like I didn't have enough or do enough. Which meant I was living with the belief that *I* was not enough.

If I could go back and talk to myself when I was in my late-teens and young adulthood, I would tell myself to have a long think about my values. I wouldn't only write down my financial goals, I would also focus on *why* I wanted to be wealthy, *how* I wanted to feel, *who* I wanted to serve and help with my success and *what*—aside from wealth—I wanted the foundation of my life built upon.

Our Core Needs: Peace, Love and Understanding

We all have three core needs: to have peace in our lives, to love and be loved and to feel understood. Our values should be moving us closer to those core needs, and there are some habits and behaviors that many of us have developed over time that become displays of our values that we're probably not aware of. Negative thoughts and motivations will never lead us to fulfillment, just like criticizing others or gossiping about them creates feelings of envy and arrogance. When you find yourself giving in to negativity, try to remember to list ten things that are positive instead. Here's an example of what I'm talking about:

Negative Behaviors That Sabotage Our Values	Positive Behaviors That Support Our Values
Greed	Service
Anger and Indifference	Compassion
Envy and Selfishness	Charity
Ego	Gratitude
Arrogance	Study and Self Reflection
Dishonesty	Integrity

When you are exploring your own definition of values, it might help to think of a prominent person in your life—a teacher, mentor, pastor, aunt or uncle—or even a famous person to use as your guiding star. Who is somebody who embodies what you want? I'm not just talking about money or status. What are their qualities? Are they confident? Are they generous? Are they smart? Are they kind? What do you admire about them?

Now, keeping in mind that no one's journey is the same as another's, study them and their success. Where did they start, and what was their path to getting to where they are now? If they are someone you can talk to, ask questions. If they're a celebrity or public figure, research them. What were their obstacles? What was their early life like, and what were they taught? Think of this as a research project—you're mapping out your own path, but you're learning about the landscape.

Have you ever seen a relief map? They are three-dimensional landscape maps created by explorers that show the elevation of the ground. Hikers and mountaineers use them to determine the elevation changes, shapes and heights of everything they'll encounter on an expedition. Think of yourself as an explorer mapping new terrain, but you want as much information as you can get about where you're going. If someone has been there, they'll know where the hills are, how steep they are, where the mountains are, where the valleys are, the rivers, streams, ponds and deserts. Even if you're blazing a new trail, the more info you have, the more successful you can be.

There's a reason the Girl Scouts' motto is "be prepared." We can't always know what to expect from life, but the more prepared we are with knowledge, information and other people's wisdom and experience, the easier the trek will be.

So before you hit the ground running to build the financial life of your dreams, let's first establish your value system so that you will be driven by a deeper desire for happiness and lasting emotional, mental and spiritual stability. You can think about what your values are as you go about your day—every time you spend money, you're making a decision about your values. Ask yourself, "What is driving this purchase?"

Chapter Two Insight Exercises

Let's determine what your values are about money and life in general. This will help you learn how to align your goals with your values so that you build a solid financial foundation, while also celebrating your wins and accomplishments along the way and finding the joy in your journey. In addition to the questions below, you might want to do some journaling around how you were raised. What were some of the earliest lessons or teachings you remember learning? What was expected of you? Is there anything you were taught in your childhood that you now reject or want to reframe?

Remember that success and happiness are not values; we often refer to them as values, but they are a product of our values and the choices we make.

. . .

Values Quiz:

1. Write out your top five values.
2. Write out five things you're most proud of in your life.
3. Write out five things you want to be remembered for after you pass away.
4. Do your current life choices reflect what you want to be remembered for?
5. What changes could you make to enjoy your life journey more? (Travel, mentoring, volunteering?)
6. What can you add to your life every day to create more value?
7. What motivates and drives you? Are you reacting to something from your past? How can you turn it into a tool?
8. How do you spend your time? How many hours in the day are you working at a job versus learning more about your industry or degree?
9. What is the *next job* you want? Is the work you're doing now moving you closer to landing that job? If not, what are some goals you can set to move in that direction?
10. In looking at your current circumstances, what could be described as an obstacle? How can you transform that into a motivator or tool? How have others overcome this or a similar obstacle?
11. What does your ideal life look like? Write five goals for the next year that are important to you. Now, next to each of those five goals, write out a timeframe to achieve the goal.

12. Under each of the goals above, write out at least three actions you must take today to reach that goal in the next 12 months.

13. Now, look at the three actions from above. Can any of those actions be transformed into a new daily routine?

14. Write out the reasons each of your goals is important to you—give them value. What feelings will arise if you don't achieve your goal? What will be the result if you don't achieve your goals?

15. Write out the feelings you will have when you *do* achieve your goals. Be specific—where are you? Who is around you? What are you wearing? An important part of manifesting the results you want is to know what that success feels like. When you walk through your day embodying those feelings, you are attracting the results you want.

For further prompts and reflections, please purchase and follow along in The Buying Time Workbook.

Chapter Three
THE CHAOS AND THE GRIND: WORK HARDER, FASTER AND SMARTER

I was an angsty teenager, causing my parents a lot of grief from 16 on up. Like a good textbook rebel teenager, I moved out of my parents' house when I was 17 and was pregnant by 19. But I refused to be a statistic: a teen mom working a dead-end job, always struggling to make ends meet.

As a teenager, I was already in my hustle to become rich, and I worked my ass off! How many 17-year-olds do you know who make 40K a year? (That may not sound like a lot today, but in 2005, it was unusual!) When I first moved out, my way of rebelling against my parents was to show them just what success looks like: I worked three jobs—I was a cheerleading and gymnastics coach, and I worked at a Joe's Crab Shack and at Round Table Pizza. Working all those hours meant I was too busy to spend what I was earning. Needless to say, my parents were amazed and surprised by my young success and drive.

Moving out of my family home the summer of 2003 between my junior and senior years of high school, I individualized at a very young age. I broke away from depending on my parents and set out to discover my life's purpose, living independently. I proved to myself and my family that having independence meant I could also achieve success. I was motivated by the belief that to have the most, you must do the most—work hard today so that eventually you won't have to work. From my teenage years, I was goal-focused. That meant I was committed to grinding today so I could live in luxury tomorrow—or someday.

The Power of Delayed Gratification

I learned early on the value of delayed gratification. To me, that seemed like the keystone to building wealth. I didn't spend the money I earned on what I considered frivolous expenses—meals out, new clothes or entertainment. Fun and shiny new "things" were a waste of money and came between me and my goals. The minute I graduated from high school, I started college. My original plan was to become an attorney. Then came a really big life change: I got pregnant.

I was 19 but I was driven, and I wasn't going to let anything slow me down. My parents announced that they were moving from the Sacramento, California area back to their home state of Utah. When I looked at my goals, I realized that the biggest challenge I would have would be achieving my goals once I had my baby. It seemed far less daunting (and less expensive) to start fresh and provide a good life for my baby if I moved with them to Utah.

We settled in Herriman, Utah, a small suburb on the Southwest side of the Salt Lake Valley. It was a newer community, and we were surrounded by other families with young kids. It was ideal for me during this time in my life because of the slower pace and lower cost of living. Many young people become attached to the idea of living in exciting, urban areas where they can be close to the "action." But with urban areas comes expensive housing and the lure of social environments that aren't compatible with a hard-working young person with big financial goals and young children!

Soon after the move, I found out that my plans of becoming a lawyer were out of reach—there was no way I could go to school, work and raise my baby. Even though my parents were completely willing to help out—my mom was willing to take care of my baby—I insisted on paying her what I would pay at a daycare. I really wanted to prove to myself that I could do it all.

I pivoted. I changed my goals and immediately started working towards my BA in business management, beginning first at a community college. My thinking was that whatever type of company I ended up working for, having a deep under-standing of how to develop policy and strategies to help that business meet its goals would make me a valuable and indis-pensable employee.

Our Most Precious Commodity: Time

Instead of attending in-person classes at the community college, I decided to enroll in online school, which allowed me to have more control over my schedule. This ended up being the best solution, as in addition to taking between 12 and 15 credits, I was also holding down two jobs while raising my child.

2006 was a big year for me. While I was working towards my degree, I not only had my baby at the age of 19, I also bought my first property—a townhouse that would be my home for years to come. The purchase price of the home was $225,000. Luckily, I only had to pay $5,000 as a down payment, as I was able to secure a specific type of loan. Then at the beginning of 2007, I got married.

By 2008, I had earned my bachelor's degree in Business

Management. I was 22 with a toddler, and because I didn't want to waste any time, I immediately started working towards getting my master's degree in accounting. I was working for a staffing agency as well as working for H&R Block helping people with their taxes. Because I was learning so much about building businesses and how money worked, I was in a hurry to start my own. By 2010, I had completed my master's degree. I was now 24, a mom of two, a home-owner and ready to start the next phase of my life.

Motivation and Goal Setting

I realize now that I was maybe an anomaly. Being a young, newlywed mom working towards a degree simply wasn't enough for me. I was also fully committed to becoming the best employee I could possibly be at both of my jobs. Looking back, I can see how I used my fears to motivate me. I turned those moments of insecurity—being stranded in the broken down car, not having money for afterschool snacks—into a tool. I decided that if I worked harder, faster and smarter than anyone else, that I could get ahead of debt, money worries and financial insecurity. Because I was so young, I was also trying to prove something to everyone in my life: that my age could not hold me back from succeeding.

Things that could have been obstacles—my age, my new baby, living on my own, moving to a new state, being a full-time student while working two jobs—were motivators. I was starting a family, and I wanted my family life to look different from what mine had been. That motivated me to get a lot done in a short amount of time.

I set goals. Some people have new year's resolutions; I had goals. To this day, I review my goals every month to monitor my progress. What kind of action can I take to move me closer to my target? Am I doing anything that could interfere with my success? What have I learned this month that can help me stay focused?

Working two jobs (while also going to school and raising a family) is exhausting—physically and mentally. You're constantly "code-switching," your brain jumping like a train from one track to another. Your trains might all be heading in the same direction towards the same goal, but they have different routes, detours, and the tracks aren't always without delays. I learned that even though I was lucky and focused, and my two jobs ultimately did lead me to achieving my goals, having multiple jobs in multiple industries can be distracting and a waste of time.

Think of it this way: having two jobs means more income, right? But getting paid by the hour means you're just trading money for time. The goal should just be to increase income, right? In the beginning, income is important, but it's not always going to be the best use of your time. When you go to school, don't miss a day and have perfect attendance, how are you rewarded? Maybe with a certificate. Sure, you've learned good discipline, which will ultimately help you in life, but does it move you ahead in any way? Now if you do not have perfect attendance, but still manage to get perfect grades, turn in extra credit, graduate top in your class—that *performance*-related reward is more valuable, as it gives you currency to get into college.

Similarly, in the workplace, showing up every day for your shift is the bare minimum, and in exchange for hours worked, you get paid. But if you show up, go above and beyond expectations, become an expert at whatever you're doing as well as an expert in what everyone else is doing, then you get noticed. Your manager will think of you first for the promotion. If there are no promotions available at your company, they will highly recommend you in a referral to another company. You will then be increasing your earning potential, getting more money for the same number of hours.

This is why I believe it's so important to stay focused on one thing and to become an expert. With just one job, you can use the extra hours in your life utilizing free resources to learn more about your industry, business, investing and managing your money.

Here are some ways to stop trading your time for money:

- *Work smarter*: get noticed for your work performance.
- *Be willing to spend money*: I went to college and grad school, but there are a lot of less traditional ways of learning about an industry or wealth-building. Nearly every city provides opportunities for real estate education, investing, day trading and stock classes. These are sometimes offered through business associations. I have compiled a list of referral partner resources on my website—these are all vetted and affordable educational programs.
- *Find free ways to learn*: YouTube is an exhaustive resource of free videos in nearly every area of learning. Granted, you have to be aware that not everyone who calls themself an expert is indeed qualified, but you can take a lesson from almost anyone.
- *Find a mentor*: Always look for someone who is in the position where you want to be. If you're starting at the bottom (like the mailroom or as a part-time employee like I was), make yourself known. Ask questions! Find someone who has what you want. Just remember that if they don't walk the walk,

they're not the right kind of coach or mentor. (For example, you want a personal trainer to be super fit, and similarly, real estate investment coaches should own over 100 properties.

- *Know when to level-up*: Recognize that there will likely come a time when you will need to level-up your coach or mentor. Once you've reached a level of success, your goals shift and change. Know how to recognize that person who has what you want *next*.

If you don't want to only take my word for it, here's what my mentor Dave Austin has to say to young people who find themselves at these pivotal moments within their lives:

Trust in yourself more and believe that you are special, even if you're different—or especially if you're different—from others. You have a special quality about you. Own that, trust in that and go forward. Know that failure is not something to worry about at an early age. I failed my way to victory. You learn as you go, so don't worry about making mistakes or failing at something. Know this world will give you opportunities to learn, so keep moving forward, because even if you don't hit your mark, you still have an opportunity to grow. That's how greatness happens. Stay the course.

Too many people are afraid to step out and take a risk because they worry about failing. Well, there is no failure by stepping out when you're learning. I don't know of any great leaders, many of whom I get to work with, who just all of a sudden became successful. They worked at it and learned through the challenges. People who have everything handed to them may appear successful, but mostly they're not, because they've never had to face adversity. Adversity propels us towards greatness.

If you see someone who appears to be a big real estate developer, they might appear to have all this money, but if you really look at their company's history, it may have gone bankrupt many times. When you look at someone who is truly successful, they've had to learn so much to move into that success. Success comes from learning from failures.

How did I have a hit record on the radio? How did I do that? I like to say, "I was bad until I was good." I was also driven and willing to deal with all the crap of not being very good. I kept moving forward and putting myself in a position so that when I actually did the record, everyone in the studio with me was a multi-platinum, big time act. I just kept moving forward. I kept learning. I surrounded myself with people better than me. I learned and grew from all that. And lo and behold, I eventually had a hit song on the radio.

Likewise, in tennis, I lost my way to winning. When I transferred to San Diego State University—that's a D-1 school—I was on scholarship as a football and baseball player. So, why in the world was I now trying to compete at tennis? I learned through the losses. Every major athlete and every successful businessperson learns through the losses.

Chapter Three Insight Exercises

Understand the value of time and make sure your efforts are always the best use of your time. Be the hardest worker in the room. There are only so many hours in a day; sometimes the best use of your time is reflecting on your success, spending time with your family or practicing some form of self-care.

Here's a quick quiz to get you thinking about your goals and actions you're taking today to move you towards them.

1. Catalog your typical day and note how many hours are dedicated to the following categories: Making Money, Personal Growth, Strengthening Relationships, Physical Health and Wellness.
2. Organize each of these categories into a wheel. Where do you see the imbalance? Remember that an uneven wheel won't roll—you need balance in every area of your life in order for your days to roll smoothly.
3. Look at the areas that are lacking satisfaction and happiness. Remember that you cannot be satisfied if you're not putting in enough effort.
4. What would your life look like if you evened out these areas (for example, six to eight hours making money, one to two hours on health)?
5. Can you still achieve your goals?
6. What can you do to bring more balance?
7. Where is the balance for you between being the hardest and the happiest worker?

For further prompts and reflections, please purchase and follow along in The Buying Time Workbook.

Chapter Four

BECOME AN EXPERT: HOW EVERYBODY'S BUSINESS IS YOUR BUSINESS

Between the years of 2010 and 2011—my husband was deployed. I would wake up at 6 am, go to my first job, go to my second job, go home to put my kids to bed, stay up doing schoolwork online until midnight, then wake up at 6 am and start all over again, day after day. I was lucky enough to have family help with child care during this time, and I don't know how I would have survived those years without that support. I never really rested. If I sat down, I was constantly checking emails and working.

My primary job was as a temporary fill-in recruiter at a staffing agency. With the energy of youth on my side, I built a reputation as the hardest working person in the room. I was like a detective. I looked at every department, every position, every role and studied it, learning every aspect of the business. I made everyone's business my business. Once I became an expert at my job, I became an expert at everyone else's and made it my job to develop an understanding of how the different departments work with each other, the function of each role and the flow of information. I didn't take a lunch break; instead I used that time to learn more. I used every opportunity given to me to learn more and to do more, and stayed focused on productivity.

I think I must have been a bit intimidating to my co-workers with my take-charge personality at such a young age—I was definitely intense! I was nosey and curious, finishing my work and then looking at everyone else's to see what needed to be done, how and why. I asked a lot of questions. I learned how the sales department corresponded to pricing and how expenses affect both. I learned how the IT department corre-lated with time management and how time spent on each task correlated to money.

During this phase of my life, I learned to celebrate being the hardest worker. I wasn't focused so much on winning anything or treating my co-workers as competition. Instead, I wanted to be known for working the hardest. That's what made me feel like I was winning. I knew deep down that as long as I was seen as reliable and focused, that if there was a prize at the end—a promotion or any other kind of professional opportunity —that I would be recognized and rewarded. This is an impor-tant lesson that I share with my kids to this day.

My second job as a tax consultant for H&R Block was initially just a way for me to justify earning my master's degree in accounting and to make a little more money. But this job ended up providing me with the most valuable on-the-job training and learning opportunities. I learned so much about money and wealth-building by looking at other people's finances, lessons I still value today and teach to my own children.

Facing Financial Literacy Head-On

A lot of people are afraid of money, numbers and math. They avoid looking at their bank accounts and tracking their spending because they don't want to face reality. They end up living well beyond their means, going into debt by maxing out credit cards paying off balances with other credit cards, and just not practicing financial hygiene. Because I was chasing success, money and financial security, looking at how other people managed or mismanaged their money was a master class in finance management. The biggest lesson I learned was how investments changed tax returns. I saw how when houses depreciate in value, investments offset your taxable income. This means that often on tax returns, these investments show up as a "negative," allowing you to pay less in taxes!

It was around this point that I started to lay the foundation for my future saving, spending and earning habits. I was clear about what I wanted and how I wanted my life to look. Unfortunately, when I married my husband, I discovered that he had about $20,000 in credit card debt. When my husband and I got married, I put myself in charge of household finances. I was determined to be debt-free, so I put together a budget and plan to save money and to pay off all of our debt. It was a hard pill to swallow, watching all of our hard-earned money go towards past purchases instead of building our future, but I had to look at everything as stages, and this was stage one.

Every month, we took $2000 from our paychecks and paid that towards the debt. We also put our credit cards in an envelope—out of sight, out of mind. If your credit cards aren't in your wallet, you use them much more thoughtfully and for emergency situations only.

The other fundamental spending habit we committed to was for every five or 10 dollars we wanted to spend here or there—on a coffee, a magazine, going through the drive-through or a manicure—we would instead ask ourselves, *"Do I need this?"* The answer was usually no, so we would *also put that money* towards our debt. While my peers were going out every night, spending their money on drinks, movies and new outfits, we were pinching pennies. As extreme and boring as this sounds, living this way meant that we paid off that $20,000 in 14 months!

Becoming Your Own Expert

The early stages of gathering information and learning about your business is also a great time to find a mentor. Find someone who has what you want—if real estate investing is your thing, maybe there's an established real estate agency in your community and one of their brokers would be willing to let you tag along on showings, look over paperwork or review listings. If you're a DJ and want to start booking gigs, why not find a local wedding planner and talk about how they book for weddings? Talk to every DJ you encounter and ask how they're booking gigs. Follow the world's most famous DJs on social media and pay close attention to how they market and promote their businesses. Follow who they follow. Contact the venues where they perform and talk to whomever books their events— ask for 15 minutes of their time and see where it goes.

The real goal here is to think outside the box and to priori-tize information gathering. Whatever it is you're pursuing, remember: you need to become an expert.

I worked two demanding jobs for three years, while raising two young kids and finishing my master's degree. When I was 23, I started working full time as a recruiter at a new staffing agency. I was earning more but also working more hours. Looking back, I wish I had found healthy ways to work smarter, because I was burning the candle at both ends. During that time, my husband and I started to set even bigger goals for ourselves, outside of our already full plates of work, long-distance marriage and parenting. My husband decided one day that he wanted to begin investing in real estate, and so we started researching the possibility of buying an investment property that we could turn into a rental.

When you're building a business of any kind, your job is to become an expert. While there are certainly a lot of free and inexpensive resources for real estate—everything from TV shows to books written by investment gurus—I do believe paying for a class in your area of interest is money very well spent. You'll learn more and make fewer mistakes (that can be expensive) along the way.

I was determined to be debt-free and to have multiple streams of income—we loved the idea of *passive* income, where we weren't just exchanging our time for money. Real estate investing was an exciting opportunity to build wealth and be business owners. As had become my routine, I knew we had to become experts at real estate investing.

We found a local real estate class that taught us the ins and outs of buying and managing rental properties. In this 12-week class, we learned how to analyze deals and how to determine if the property we were considering was a good deal based on comparable recent sales in the area as well as upcoming trends. We were taught all the details involved in buying properties, all about the paperwork and the closing costs involved. We also learned about what types of properties we should remodel and how to then refinance the property into long-term financing. Once we were confident with our newly-learned skills, we dove in and bought our first property together in 2012 right after my 25th birthday. Right away, I was hooked.

The Compounding Growth of Enthusiasm

What started as a simple, one-property plan quickly grew into something more in my mind. I saw the potential of this becoming a solid wealth-building industry, and I wanted to build a real estate portfolio. We had planted a seed, and I saw before us an entire garden of investment opportunities and a real foundation for a future of financial freedom. This was the answer to how I could have multiple streams of income, and this way I wouldn't be trading dollars for my time—it would be mostly passive income building.

I felt like I was starting to see a very promising future ahead of me. My successes were feeding my drive; we had not only paid off our debt in a short amount of time, we had purchased a townhouse, built a substantial savings account allowing us to buy a property, and I was quickly developing a deeper understanding of how to run a staffing agency. As you can tell, I am a very goal-oriented person. I set each goal like a target, and all my focus and energy goes to keeping my aim on that target until I achieve the goal. I'm always thinking, "What's next?" I'm premeditating my next move even as I'm finishing the tasks in front of me.

There are two pivotal decisions I made at this time that truly launched me in the direction of becoming a successful entrepreneur at a young age. The first decision was that I was going to double down on my real estate goals every year. One property would become two, which would become four, and on until I'd built a real estate empire.

The second decision I made was to launch my own staffing company. Because I had now spent years learning about every role and every aspect of this industry, by 2015, I was ready. I had worked for other people long enough, and the time had come for me to put into practice how to be the entrepreneur I was dying to be.

Chapter Four Insight Exercises

I wish I had learned to live in the present moment and to really value each moment. Also, a lot of people work several jobs in various industries to create more income. In the beginning, income is important, but you have to master something. Jobs (or two or three!) are important for skill building, learning, income and relationship development.

Answer the following questions for yourself:

1. How is your job in line with your goals?
2. If you work eight hours a day, how many of those hours are of value to your goals?
3. How many hours a day are you working towards becoming an expert in the field of your dreams?
4. How many hours each day are you watching TV or scrolling through social media when you could be building valuable skills?
5. Map out the company you work for by department. Do you know how the different departments interact?
6. Make a list of the various roles at your place of work. Now strategize: whose job are you going to learn about first?
7. Who could be your mentor?

For further prompts and reflections, please purchase and follow along in The Buying Time Workbook.

Chapter Five
HOW MONEY WORKS (AND HOW TO MAKE IT WORK FOR YOU)

Before we move on to the ins and outs of building a business and becoming a millionaire entrepreneur, I want to take some time to explain how money works. This is all information I have learned throughout my business-building career that I wish I had known before I started. I figured these things out on the fly as I moved from one stage to the next, but I want to save you some time! I have learned this information from classes, workshops, institutions of higher learning, from mentors, from industry leaders, from coaches, from gurus, from CEOs, from books and, most importantly, from my own mistakes.

This is all information that should, in my opinion, be taught in or before high school. There are too many of us growing up with fear of money and a lack of understanding about how it works; how to manage it, how to save it and how to grow it. I want every young person to know this information before they "go out into the world." I want you to start your young adulthood strong, responsible and ready to earn.

If you've already started working—whether it's at a McDonald's or as an intern at your uncle's car dealership—this info is for you.

If you're going off to college and have signed up for Econ 101, this info is for you.

If you dropped out of high school, are a young parent and don't feel like there's any hope of you ever living beyond paycheck to paycheck, this info is for you.

If you're still in high school and want more than you have today, this info is for you.

Mastering Financial Hygiene

In this chapter, we'll be covering 10 easy-to-follow steps anyone can take towards developing good "financial hygiene," or healthy habits that will help set the stage for lifelong success. Think about it: you brush your teeth every day, shower or take a bath, wear deodorant, wash your face, put on lotion. These are hygiene habits you formed when you were young to take care of yourself and keep your body healthy. Financial hygiene is a vital part of keeping your *life* healthy. (As an aside, there is also a chapter in this book a little later about mindset—ways to keep your thinking healthy. It all matters!)

If you develop these financial hygiene skills now, in the early years of your business-building, you can avoid a lot of mental anguish throughout life that comes as a side effect of not knowing how to handle your money. Financial hygiene is just another way of explaining healthy attitudes, habits and actions you can take that keep you moving forward towards your goals, and to keep you feeling fearless and in control of what you earn and what you spend.

As I've explained, I was incredibly motivated and focused at a really young age—maybe *too* focused. I was motivated by fear. Fear of not having enough, fear of being poor and fear of not being in control of my money and life. While this fear ended up helping me to build a solid financial life, I wish I could have experienced more joy during these years. Every waking minute, I was working and thinking about what more I could do. This is not my hope for you.

My hope is for you to feel *free* from a young age. *Free* of fear because you are empowered by financial wisdom and confidence. That confidence will come from a place of understanding that you are taking all the right steps towards a bright financial future by starting these healthy habits now.

1. Educate Yourself

I went to a community college and got my bachelor's degree in Business Management, then my master's degree in Accounting. To me, this was the best way to build a foundation of knowledge based on the established rules of success. My jobs at the time were completely in line with these degrees, so I was practicing what I was learning *while* I was learning.

College is not for everyone. It's not always the best path, and I believe in and endorse alternate life courses. Some people are daunted by going into debt for an education, struggle with learning challenges or have too many life responsibilities to be taking a full load of classes. (Having said that, I was a mom, working multiple jobs while attending college, so please know that anything is possible!) But getting a college degree is *not* the only way to succeed, and it often means taking on what feels like insurmountable debt.

You don't have to follow my path, or anyone else's path, to learning what you need to know in order to succeed. However, you do need to look for every opportunity to learn. You don't have to enroll as a full-time, matriculated student—you can enroll in any community college part time! You can take only the classes that interest you versus working towards a degree. But I will say that having a degree makes you more of an *expert* in your field, with the framed diploma on the wall that will give you and your colleagues confidence in your knowledge and training.

Two- or four-year colleges aren't the only paths to learning in a class setting. You can sign up for a single class at any community college and elsewhere to learn about investing, real estate, accounting, taxes, money management, business management, starting an LLC or C-Corporation, or any other type of industry-related topic. Many cities have associations (business, real estate, women in business and more) that offer classes and workshops for very little money that would be an invaluable learning opportunity for you (try these websites for resources: slreia.com, utahreia.com and uvreia.com). Aside from my college courses, I also took classes on day trading and how to invest in stocks. I made sure that the person teaching the class had what I wanted: experience investing in stocks and success in day-trading, and they had built significant wealth doing so.

These classes are also great places to meet mentors. By showing up and showing your enthusiasm for learning, others will take an interest in you. Show that you are eager, and your attitude will be contagious—others will be eager to help you!

There are also endless online learning courses and opportunities in almost any field of expertise you can imagine. Seminars and webinars have really taken off as ways for experts to reach people all over the world. Many coaches and teachers offer a free introductory class to their programs that give you a taste of what you can expect if you sign up for their full course of study. Some of these can be expensive, so I would learn everything you can for *free* before signing up for a more expensive program that you may not be ready for.

As an example, it would be better to learn about setting up an LLC before you sign up for a real estate investing course— that way, by the time you've learned about real estate investing, you can hit the ground running with the LLC already formed! Another example would be to learn everything you can about filing taxes when you are an LLC owner *before* forming your LLC, so that you aren't playing catch-up and making mistakes at tax time. That would be a very scary time to find out that you should have been setting money aside all along to pay your taxes!

There are also many free learning opportunities online. I can't tell you how much I've learned by simply googling a topic, and finding an endless number of videos with experienced investors, business leaders, CEOs and teachers who have no problem sharing their knowledge for free. My suggestion here would be to watch as much as you can by as many content creators as possible so that you can take the good from each of them. Keep in mind that anyone can call themselves an "expert," but without really knowing their success rate, experience, business acumen or education, you shouldn't follow just anyone's advice. Sometimes things are worth what we pay for them—and free isn't always worth more than that.

By taking classes to learn about the areas of business-building and investing that you don't already understand, you are taking powerful steps towards building your own business. Never go into a venture thinking you already know everything! To this day, after building multiple, multi-million dollar companies, I never go into any situation assuming I already know everything, as every deal and opportunity is different. There is always someone who is smarter, more savvy and more successful than me.

But keep in mind that free information isn't always reliable. Finding a mentor is important, but finding the *right* mentor or coach is invaluable. Once you have a little money, I absolutely recommend investing in yourself, your ideas and your future by investing in a coach or mentor with expertise in your field. One primary reason for this is you want to be taken seriously by your mentor—if you're just hanging around asking questions, they're only willing to give you so much for free—they're not going to invest in you because there's no return on their investment. You may be delightful, but successful people know better than to invest their time and energy into someone who is not serious about following their advice. The mentor-mentee relationship is ideally one where the mentee eventually surpasses the mentor in their success! You will be out in the world representing them, so they'll value your relationship more if they see you are also investing in them.

This is different if your mentor is someone at the place where you work. Your employer already sees promise in you because they hired you! They are already investing in you and your future, because your success is tied to their success. If you are proving your worth in the workplace, they'll see you as someone who wants to help them succeed. If you want to be the best, find who you think is the best, and pay them to invest in making you the best you can be.

It's going to take a lot more than reading one book to become a successful entrepreneur (though you're obviously smart enough to have picked up this one!). Remember, you need to *make everyone's business your business!* That means treat *learning* as your business, and never stop learning.

2. Budget!

Most people *dread* the word budget. People like to have money and spend the money they have. When a paycheck rolls in, they immediately start spending—buying things they've had on their list since their last paycheck. Or they go out and celebrate getting paid! How many people do you know who go out on payday to a club or restaurant, throwing money around like it's a never-ending fountain of cash? Drinks and food at multiple bars, new outfits for the night out and car services from home then to every other stop, trying to catch up with friends.

Budgeting does *not* mean never having fun. I learned that the hard way. I was so focused on the grind that I never stopped to enjoy the process. Sure, I did really enjoy building my businesses, but I can't say I had a lot of fun in my 20s! While I was building and saving, I think I could have set aside a little bit of money to enjoy my life more. I could have had more balance during this time in my life. I was surrounded by peers my own age in school, but I didn't really ever go out to celebrate the little wins with them—like celebrating when finals were over, or even just meeting up after class to learn a bit about each other. I live differently now, and while "delaying gratification" is still one of my most valuable financial hygiene rules, I think having a budget line for entertainment is important.

Living with a budget is knowing how much is coming in, what your daily expenses are, how much you need to pay bills and knowing how to not overspend—or spend on items you don't need.

As I've mentioned, my husband and I very quickly paid off $20,000 in debt in just 14 months by making it our first priority. We were able to do this because we had a budget and a plan.

3. Pay Off Debt

Debt is terrifying. For so many people, their debt grows faster than their savings, and life can begin to feel hopeless, as it seems impossible to tackle that debt while also dealing with day-to-day expenses and bills.

The easiest answer is this: don't accrue debt. What most young people don't know is that they are targets. Credit card companies count on you having very little understanding of how money works, so they target college fairs and campuses, hoping to get young and naive recruits to sign up for "free money." I can't tell you how many twenty-something-year-olds I meet who are already drowning in debt from credit card expenses.

Credit cards are very enticing. It seems as though using a card today to cover a dinner out will be super easy to pay for next month when we have more money! Or we negotiate with ourselves, saying "just this once, I have to have fun, right?" So many credit cards also offer things like "cash back," low APRs or airline miles—any number of bonus freebies if you sign on the line today! Paying with a credit card makes you feel rich. It doesn't feel like your money, because *it's not.*

Before we know it, as happened with my husband, you feel like you're running from tens of thousands of dollars that can't be paid off no matter how hard you try, you can barely make the minimum payment each month, and you have too much shame around it to face it and pay it off.

Here's what worked for us: every day, we chose not to spend money on something we didn't need. We'd ask ourselves, "Is this a *need* or a *want?*" We would only spend money on something that was a *need,* and we'd put the money we *would have* spent towards our debt–then once the debt was paid off, we would put that money instead into savings. We also put our credit cards into an envelope—by doing this, we really had to go through a lot of effort and discussion to open the envelope and use that credit card. So we didn't.

We looked at our combined income, our bills—utilities, car payments and the townhouse mortgage—and after that was spent, we put the rest towards debt. This ended up being about $2000 per month, just $10 at a time—not much! But living this way, that debt was *gone* after just over a year. Once that debt was paid off, I can't tell you how free we felt!

Once our debt was paid off, we continued to put the money we would otherwise be throwing towards the debt into a savings account. This is the ultimate in exercising delayed gratification. By not spending money on things we didn't need, we got to not only celebrate the *major* win of being debt free, but we also got the gratification of having a healthy savings account that helped us become investors.

4. Start Saving

A savings account can sometimes feel impossible, especially when you're living paycheck to paycheck. So many people experience the feeling of watching their entire paycheck go towards rent or mortgage, bills and utilities, leaving nothing to set aside. But I'm here to tell you *anyone* can have a savings account, even a small one.

How you contribute to a savings account, how much you contribute and how often is personal. Like I mentioned before, we created a savings account by first getting out of debt (if we made more money, we could have put more than $2000 per month towards that debt and paid it off faster), then putting that same amount into a savings account once we were debt-free. We looked at every single dollar and asked ourselves if we *had to* spend it. If it wasn't a required expense, that money went into savings instead.

Starting a savings account when you are young—like in middle school or high school—is one of the best ways to get ahead. Typically, teenagers really don't have any expenses! You're not paying rent or for utilities, so any money you make— babysitting, working a part-time job or birthday gifts—can go directly into a savings account. The bare minimum of financial commitment you can make to yourself right now is to put *at least* 50 percent of your income into savings. If you don't have a lot of living expenses—you don't pay rent, have car payments or need to pay for utilities—then you can put way more money directly into savings. Then by the time you graduate, you're already ahead! I had my own children always save 50 percent of their income since they were about five years old. Every dollar they got for a lemonade stand, for a chore or as a gift from a relative, they only got to spend half and the other half went into savings. By doing this, my oldest saved $7,000 during the summer between his sophomore and junior years of high school! He felt so accomplished and is so excited to put that money to good use someday.

Imagine if you babysit a neighborhood kid twice a week. You charge their parents $15 per hour, and each shift is about three hours. That's $45 twice a week, so $90 a week, which means $360 a month! And you're too young to pay taxes, so that's tax-free money! After a year of saving this money instead of spending it at the movies, the mall or in-app purchases, you will find yourself with $4,320 dollars. And if your savings account pays you interest, that's even more. If you do this for three years (10th, 11th and 12th grades), by the time you graduate, you will have at least $12,960 in your savings account, which is well on your way to making your first investment.

It's never too early to start saving. I started my kids when they were babies! If you are a parent, here's a clever trick to set your kids on a path towards financial success later in life: a Whole Life Insurance Investment Strategy!

Insurance premiums are cheaper when people are younger. Instead of investing in a 529 Plan where they can only use the funds for college, the whole life insurance policy allows my kids to take out a loan against the cash value of their policy when they turn 18. That loan will allow them to buy a four-plex apartment unit where they can live while collecting money on the other three units. That income pays their rent every month and then some. They can also use the money from the whole life insurance policy to start a business. When you take out a loan against the policy's value, your policy will still continue to grow and will be invested at its value before they took out a cash loan against it. Also, the investment grows tax free.

I also contribute to a Roth IRA for each of my kids that grows tax free and can be transferred to a self-directed IRA which they can also use for investments in the future; this will continue to grow and will be tax free.

5. Make Your Money Grow

So now you have a bit of a savings account. What are the best ways to make this money grow? How can you put your money to work for you, providing a passive investment? Money is just like dieting. When we aren't tracking what we eat or focus on macros, we eat too much and gain weight. Similarly, when we aren't disciplined and tracking our finances, we spend money on unnecessary things, five dollars at a time, and end up living paycheck to paycheck. Once you know what you're making and where your money is going, you can make more conscious decisions about how you are spending, and put money into savings before you even see it. I always recommend setting up a savings account at a bank on the other side of town–without a debit card–so you won't be tempted to access that money! You're protecting your assets from yourself, and your money will be growing out of sight and out of mind. Then when you check it annually, you'll be investing it into something with a higher return.

Investing options are dependent on your risk tolerance—which means how you feel about high versus low risk investments. If the risk of losing money makes you nervous, you are "low risk." If you get excited by the potential returns on an investment, even if you might lose some money in the process, then you are "high risk" tolerant. For low-risk tolerance, start out with investing in CDs, the stock market or safe mutual funds. As you grow your savings, you can take a little more risk and choose to invest in riskier stocks or real estate. As mentioned above, a whole life insurance policy is a no-risk, great long-term growth plan that has a higher rate of returns than a traditional savings account.

6. Manage Cash Flow

If you've started making some money (whether from babysitting, mowing lawns or flipping burgers), you have to understand how to create and maintain a balance sheet. Remember, I went to school for accounting, so this is my expertise.

One thing I learned early on is the importance of keeping business profits separate from my personal spending accounts. When I made any profit in my investments (for example, my first investment property that became a rental), I didn't touch or spend any of that profit. I put it all into a business account that

I used only for investing. As that account grew, believe me—I was tempted to spend it! Who wouldn't want to spend money instead of just letting it sit there? But I had to acknowledge that I was at the very beginning of building my business, and I couldn't live like I was "successful" yet. I decided that I had to be disciplined in my 20s while I was just starting out so that I could enjoy myself later in my 30s, 40s, 50s and 60s—and on and on, building a legacy for my kids and future generations.

Remember that real estate investing was not my only money stream; I also had a job! I used my income as a recruiter to live on and treated my properties as a hands-off-future-building business. But by now you know that I was very serious about building wealth, so I *also* took half of my income from my recruiter job and invested *that* in my real estate business. Reinvest your profit back into your business, and watch your wealth grow. It is important to stay disciplined with your budget even after you have some financial stability. By managing your cash flow and continually reinvesting your profits, you have more money to work with and can invest in higher return options that have a more expensive entry point.

7. Grow Your Business, Whatever It Is

Let's use the babysitting model I mentioned before. Every single neighborhood and school district has an endless stream of parents with young kids who are desperate for help. Sometimes it's walking kids home from school and helping them with homework. Sometimes they need someone to take them to their activities. Sometimes the parents need a date night or have an important meeting. How can you turn this into a business opportunity?

Start with understanding the need: parents want to know

that they're hiring someone reliable and responsible. You have to establish yourself as the favorite neighborhood sitter by collecting excellent references and referrals from every family you work for. You have to show up on time, you have to do what's asked of you, and you have to go above and beyond what's being asked of you.

Sure, it's really easy to pick a kid up from elementary school and walk them home, turn on the TV and collect your money after a couple of hours. But what if you instead used that time to work on their soccer or softball skills? Showed them how to do algebra, how to code, make homemade cookies or to write a short story? Their parents will see you as someone who is invested in their child, therefore making *their child your business.* If you become an expert in that family's needs, you are developing a business.

Before you know it, the Smith family is telling the Jones family that they have the best babysitter in town! You find families competing for your services, and eventually, you can ask for more money. If you're working with two kids instead of one, that's more money. Maybe the Smith family has one child and the Jones family has one child, and you charge them $15 per hour *each child* to take them to the park and play soccer? You've doubled your rates!

There is a group of high school girls in my community who have created a babysitting collective. They launched a website with profiles for each available babysitter, including their age, skills, references, rates and availability. What's more is they've all vowed to donate a certain percentage of each shift to a charitable organization. They have become experts in their field of business, advertising on social media through their own parents and other families in various community groups. This is a valuable community resource that every family is desperate for.

Many families and the elderly also need help with pet care—whether it's a daily walk or two, or feeding or caring for a pet while they are on vacation. Not everyone can afford the expensive kenneling day or overnight rates, but they can afford to pay a reliable young person to come to their house once a day for a walk, fresh water and a couple scoops of food! Make sure you maintain great relationships with your clients, and they'll happily provide you with references and referrals to help you build your business.

These are just a couple examples of how a young entrepreneur can start a business to meet a need, and build a savings account that will help them hit the ground running by the time they're 18 and ready for the next phase of building on their business and growing their savings.

My first business of choice made itself very clear to me. Once I got a taste of investing in real estate, I wanted more. I made a commitment to grow my business one property at a time by *doubling* my efforts each time. By putting all my profit into one account that I wasn't touching, I watched it grow until I had enough to make my next investment. I set lofty goals for myself. My first goal was one investment property. My next goal was *two* investment properties. I continued to double my goals. Because of how much money I was investing in my property ownership business—the profit from each home as well as half of my paycheck—by the end of 2013, I had four investment properties plus my townhouse. At this time, we decided to turn the townhouse into another rental property.

I'll go into more detail on this real estate business-building model later in the book, but here is the basic strategy of how I grew my business:

- I put half of my paycheck from my recruiter job into my business account.

- I also put all of my profits from my investment properties into that business account and didn't touch it.
- I used that business account to purchase another property, and another and another, until I had four.

This snowballing technique is the key to building a business. Take all the profit from your business to grow your business and live on 50 percent of your income. A huge mistake people make is that they spend more as they make more. We could have moved out of the townhouse into a single family home a lot earlier, but we chose to instead use those funds to grow our rental portfolio and business so that when we chose to move out of townhouse, we could still save half of our income. Moving sooner would have cut into our savings goal and ultimately our business growth.

8. Let Your Assets Pay the Bills

What are assets? In the example of real estate, it's easy to see that the properties you own are your assets. The money you make from those properties—that is any surplus after you've paid the mortgage and any other associated bills or expenses—is profit. You put the profit into an account and let it sit there to be used *only* for expenses related to this business.

Having tenants means having expenses—you have to make sure the roof isn't leaking, that the dishwasher is working and that the air conditioner works in the summer. Maybe you're great at fixing things yourself, but if not, you'll be paying someone else to be making these repairs.

You also have the responsibility of making sure you have reliable tenants, because you lose money every time one moves out. You have to do repairs on the property, sometimes do upgrades on appliances and paint the walls every time someone moves out. There's also yard maintenance and other expenses—you will pay for all of these things out of the business account.

After nine years of working as a recruiter for a staffing agency, I decided it was time to start my own agency. I had learned everything there was to know about the industry in my years working for other people, so I was also very clear on how to make this business a success—and it's a good thing I did, because I wore many, many hats in those first years of building this business.

Most people buy cars and toys, and often take out loans from lenders (banks or car dealerships) to pay for those items. Imagine if instead of putting down $5,000 as a payment towards a car, and every $5 you spend on toys, that you instead saved a bit longer and *bought a rental house.* The thing about cars is that they depreciate in value the moment they leave the lot. Over time, they depreciate even more with wear and tear. And those little toys you spend $5 or $20 on here or there? Most of them end up broken or forgotten within six months. But if you take that money and buy a property instead, the profit on that rental will *pay your car payment.* Not only is this the same out-of-pocket expense, it fulfills the same need—a car —it also helps when it comes time to pay taxes. When you buy assets instead of toys, you are investing rather than spending, but the money leaving your wallet is the same.

9. Become Profitable

Regardless of the business you are starting, there will be a period of time where you're learning about all the different roles, and where your strengths and stretches are. In the early days of my staffing agency, I wore what I now know to be "too many hats." I was the CFO, the Operations Manager, Human Resources, the hiring manager and so on. As I learned, it's very normal to feel overwhelmed in the early days of business-building, no matter how prepared and educated you are—and in a short amount of time, I learned the value of hiring other people to take over jobs that fit their expertise. This is true from one type of business to another. In property ownership, I learned quickly that I'm not a plumber, an electrician or even a painter! I learned that one expense of business-building is hiring the right people to fill the right roles, to get the job done correctly the first time.

I am a big proponent of delayed gratification. When we opened our staffing business, we could have paid ourselves a ton of money every month. But if we had done that, we would not have had the cash flow in the business to expand and grow our profits. Instead, we opted to pay ourselves less, while both contributing to our savings and investing our profit into multiple markets and hiring more employees. We created a formula where 25 percent of our profits went into a tax account, 20 percent went into a savings account and the remaining 5 percent of profit was distributed to the owners. In doing this, we left money in the business allowing it to grow faster. Had we distributed that money, we would not have had the funds to increase our workforce and the number of states we could cover. We knew that by increasing our workforce, we increased our revenue.

I applied this same practice to my real estate investing; I never took money out of that business, and instead let it compound into bigger and more profitable projects.

10. Align Your Job with Your Goals

Having a job or two (or three!) is great in the early stages of starting a business and putting the learning process in fast motion. As I've mentioned, I had various stages of life where I had two and three jobs. This was also key to me paying for college and graduate school. I was very lucky that all my hard work as a recruiter allowed me to transition to a new job at a new agency. Because of all that I was learning in this career, I could see a pathway to owning my own staffing agency. My job was an investment in my big-picture entrepreneurial goals. I was getting on-the-job business-building training because the work I was doing (and getting paid for!) was in line with my goals.

Imagine for a moment that I spent those years working part-time at a doctor's office as a receptionist. I would certainly have learned a lot! But unless my goals were to become a doctor someday and to have my own practice, I wouldn't have been moving towards my goals. Similarly if I were working as a paralegal, I would maybe have made more money per hour, but unless I want to become a lawyer, court reporter or judge, it would not have been as smart of an investment in *me*.

My jobs—both as a recruiter and doing taxes for H&R Block—were completely in line with my big-picture goals of owning my own staffing agency some day and being an investor. Take some time to map out your own entrepreneurial dreams, and brainstorm about the types of jobs you can pursue now that move you closer to achieving those goals. Learn everything you can about your industry, and know that you are investing in your future, building a foundation for success.

Chapter Five Insight Exercises

One thing I did early in my business-building journey was to educate myself on investments *while* I was paying off debt. Even though I wasn't in a position to invest anything just yet, I was able to hit the ground running once my debt was taken care of. I took real estate investing courses and day trading lessons so there was little to no lag time between eliminating our debt and implementing our investment strategies. Just because our debt was paid off, that didn't mean we suddenly changed our spending or saving habits—all the money we had been putting towards debt was now going into savings.

1. Write down everything you know about investing. Where did you learn it?
2. What are you interested in investing in? Real estate, stocks, day trading, other types of investing?
3. Looking at each of these categories, what resources can you use to develop a deeper understanding of each? Where can you take classes or watch tutorials?
4. Who do you know who has successfully invested in each of these areas? Try to find someone who is successful in the industry where you want to succeed, and ask them to mentor you. Take them for coffee, and find out if they're willing to share their knowledge and experience with you.
5. Where can you take classes to learn more about what interests you? There are real estate associations in most cities with a very low yearly membership fee that you can join that will give you access to experts in your area. For maybe $100 a

year, you can get unlimited amounts of valuable information and advice.

6. Look for social media groups where you can ask experts all your questions to help you get ahead. Some of these are official associations, and some are agents who stay in touch and talk about trends in their communities. These groups are free and can be a great resource!

For further prompts and reflections, please purchase and follow along in The Buying Time Workbook.

Chapter Six
THE PAYOFF

My early 20s were about grinding. I worked multiple jobs while raising multiple children. I was intentionally laying the foundation for my financial future, and I was very focused on a future with wealth beyond my dreams. Even though I was gradually making more money than ever, I was still living a frugal lifestyle instead of taking extravagant vacations, wearing designer clothes and driving expensive cars.

My early success at such a young age was due to my willingness to follow directions—at work and with my coaches and mentors. I also had a good amount of hustle; I was patient, disciplined and took regular action in the direction of my goals. I was assertive, and I consistently used my time efficiently.

With my schedule of doing homework and going to work at one of my jobs, I was always looking for ways to save time. I'll never forget the early years when my kids and I would put our clothes directly into the washing machine at the end of the day instead of the laundry hamper—then when the machine was full, I would run it right away, instead of wasting time with gathering and sorting! Even my three-year-old knew how to put dirty dishes into the dishwasher immediately after eating! I taught my kids at a very young age how to be economical with their time. This is part of financial hygiene, especially when you're first building your future. We also saved time and money by canceling our cable subscription. We weren't sitting around watching TV—we used that valuable time to earn and save money.

My family and I continued to live in our townhouse in Utah, and we expanded our rental property business one property at a time. I should note that nearly all of our investment properties were nicer than the townhouse we were living in! This was an easy sacrifice to make, because I was seeing the benefits of my frugality and following my primary rule: delaying gratification.

Adventures in Real Estate and Business

We were living in an inexpensive property and paid off our debt quickly. Our next important money decision was to take the same amount of money we were directing to our debt and instead contribute that same amount to our savings account. We didn't reward ourselves for paying off debt—no big celebratory steak dinner and no shopping spree. Instead, we maintained our frugal lifestyle so that inside of a year, we had $20,000 in savings.

We purchased our first rental property and contributed all of the money we made each month in profit *plus* half of our income into a separate account that we didn't touch. With that savings, I was ready to build upon our first investment property and to grow my real estate business.

I was so thrilled with the results of achieving my first goal—owning a rental property. My next move was to double my goal—going from one rental property, then buying two. By 2013, we had four rental properties. We continued to follow our money, budget and savings rules, and focused on building our investment property portfolio. I was feeling confident, successful and really energized by owning my own business. With confidence comes a willingness to take a bigger swing—I felt the urge to make a leap into a higher-stakes opportunity. To me, the next logical step was to do what a lot of very successful real estate investors do—I bought my first "flip."

If you watch any of those real estate shows, you know how easy they make it look. Buy a cheap property priced below market value, put a little money into it, fix it up and then sell it for more money—at or slightly above market. Buyers love a move-in ready home that is often the nicest on the block. Count your money and repeat! I'm sure you see "We buy ugly houses!" fliers in your community. There are people everywhere who want to purchase run-down properties, fix them up and flip them.

A "flip" is essentially the act of buying a home as a short-term business opportunity with no intention of using it as a long-term investment (as you would with a rental property). The ultimate goal is to put as little money into the property as possible, own it only long enough to make it nicer, and then sell it above the purchase price, making a healthy profit. Many flips can happen inside of a year—if you are disciplined and know your numbers inside and out. And it helps if you are very, very skilled.

But with flips comes work that not everyone has the skills to complete. By "everyone," I mean *me*. There was painting, demolition, construction, building supplies, remodeling work, inspections, permits, the purchasing paperwork and more. Have you ever heard the saying, "don't trip over a dime to pick up a penny?" I thought that by doing all this work myself, I could save time and money. Instead of hiring experts to do the work, I did it myself, and I didn't do it well.

My flip became a failure. The time and money I put into that house was a waste. I was putting a second coat of paint on cabinets when I should have been spending my time at one of my other jobs *earning* money. I should have paid someone else —an expert who knew what they were doing—for the labor, despite the out of pocket expense. In the end, that first flip *cost me* $52,000.

My ego was bruised. I worked harder than anyone I knew, and this was my first real flop. I wasn't used to losing! I had made a very expensive series of bad decisions. As funny as it sounds, I hope that *you too* make similar mistakes! Whatever you endeavor to do, there is a risk of failure. Failures are education, and I decided to treat this as a $52,000 doctorate's degree in an area of business that was new for me. I now had a PhD in Failed Flips, and I wouldn't make those mistakes again.

Nursing my wounds, I took some time to focus on my other areas of income earning. My rental properties were successful, and I had continued to master my role as a recruiter at the staffing agency. In 2015, the year I turned 28, I took another leap: I started my own staffing company.

I now had two steady and reliable streams of income, and I continued following my healthy financial hygiene rules of taking half my income and contributing it to my real estate investing company.

Eventually, we moved out of the townhouse and rented it out—creating another source of income. We purchased a house —a fixer-upper near my mom's house—and over the years have renovated the entire thing, turning it into the house of my dreams, complete with new landscaping and a pool. We used a VA loan to purchase it, which requires zero money down. However, not everyone has access to options like the VA loan. Luckily, there are strategies commonly used by real estate investors that make it possible for you to build your investment portfolio without spending all of your personal savings.

"Equity" is the difference between the market value of a property and the amount owed on the mortgage. For example, if a property is worth $300,000 and the mortgage balance (the outstanding money owed on the bank loan) is $200,000, the equity in this property is $100,000. You can use that equity as the funds for purchase of another property.

The benefit of leveraging one property against another is that you're increasing the return on your investment, allowing you to buy more properties with less money out of your own pocket. This increases the potential income and appreciation (the increase in value) from the properties, and also creates opportunities for tax benefits and business deductions. These investments also diversify your portfolio, allowing you to buy different types of properties—which can reduce any risks of normal market fluctuations. Of course, the more properties you own, the more you increase your business and financial growth.

To leverage one property against another, you can use a few different methods:

1. *Take out a home equity loan*: This loan allows you to access a portion of the equity in your property as a lump sum (in the example above, a portion of that $100,000). This loan has a fixed interest rate and a fixed repayment agreement. You can use that money to buy another property (or for any purpose

—but remember, keep your business money in your business!). Just remember that a home equity loan is a second mortgage that adds to the existing debt on the property.

2. *A home equity line of credit (HELOC)*: This is a revolving line of credit that allows you to access the equity in your property as needed. You can draw funds (up to a certain limit) and pay interest only on the amount used, and you can use that money for buying another property. But remember: a HELOC is also a second mortgage that adds to the existing debt on the property.

3. *A cash-out refinance*: This is the process of replacing the existing mortgage with a new one that has a higher balance. You can use the difference between the old and new loan amounts to buy another property or for any other purpose. A cash-out refinance may have a lower interest rate than a home equity loan or HELOC, but it also resets the repayment agreement and may increase the monthly payments.

There are risks involved in leveraging one property against another, and I would definitely advise you to work with a coach who really understands real estate law and investing so you can look together at your unique situation to make the right decision for you. Without knowing how to navigate these decisions, you risk losing both properties. The reason for this is that by using equity as collateral, you put your original property at risk of foreclosure if you fail to make the payments on the loan (home equity loan, HELOC or cash-out refinance). Another risk is that you reduce your liquidity and flexibility by locking up any equity in that additional property and incurring higher monthly expenses. You're no longer able to access that equity as cash in case of emergencies (like damage to one of your other properties) or other investment opportunities. You also are limited in your ability to sell or refinance your original property should you need to. You are ultimately increasing your debt and expenses by adding more debt to your original property, while also increasing your monthly payments and interest costs, as well as maintenance, taxes, insurance and management fees.

Internal and External Transformation

Because I was feeling confident in my real estate strategies, my business growth and my successful staffing agency, I rewarded myself and started buying nicer cars. The good news is that even though you are frugal and saving money everywhere you can, you can still have nice things! Here's my rule: if you can't afford to buy that "something nice" (jewelry, a nice car, a new home) and *still invest in your business*, that purchase is too expensive. Whatever payments you have must make sense with your budgeting and allow you to continue to save and maintain your upward momentum.

In 2018, I mustered the courage and made the big decision to try a second flip. Having learned from my expensive mistakes, I was determined to do it right. I hired experts—a contractor, painters, plumbers and electricians to do the work I was not skilled enough to do. Even by paying others out of pocket for the labor, this time I made $45,000 in profit. Meeting that goal, I once again doubled my goal—I did two more flips immediately. I lumped all of the profits from these flips together then I did four flips at a time, then five—eventually doing 12 flips in one year!

I learned my lessons about hiring the right people with expertise for specific jobs. This is true in my flipping business as well as my staffing agency. I filled all the important positions at my company with the best candidates available—experts who could hit the ground running, helping me to build my business and make it successful.

I started my new business as an expert in the industry because of all I had learned first as a recruiter for four years at one agency, then five more years as a full-time recruiter at another. This is the value of making everyone else's business your business in a position that is in line with your goals. I understood the industry I was working in, and I understood each position at the agency and how departments worked together to achieve company-wide goals. I knew what to look for in employees and staff and how to recognize experts. Within two years of launching my business, it was worth over $10 million dollars.

But what is even more important than my business and wealth-building success was that my inner life was changing too. The way I was responding to external circumstances was evolving. I was responding differently in my personal and professional relationships. I was learning that I didn't have to react to every little thing happening in my life, and I didn't have to take what other people did or said personally. Even with my husband and his bouts of trauma-related outbursts, I was learning to stay calm. Previously, I would treat every upsetting situation as a big, dramatic emergency that demanded an equally huge response from me—that's how I validated its importance. Now I was focused on staying in my serenity no matter what the situation I was finding myself in. I was learning to de-escalate instead of escalating the challenge with my own heated emotions.

Another area where I noticed this change in me taking place was on the road. We've all experienced road rage in varying degrees of extremes. Someone cuts me off, takes my parking spot, merges without a signal—and bam! My blood pressure and anger would be through the roof! But as I became better at recognizing situations that were outside of my control, I didn't feel the need to give them more energy. I was keeping my cool, and instead thinking to myself, "I guess that person didn't see me!" or "they're really in a hurry, let me just stay out of their way to be safe." This inner transformation was showing up in my life in small and large ways. I was consciously choosing to act from a place of love instead of emotion. This change has been the real payoff of all my years of hard work— the work I'm doing on myself.

Chapter Six Insight Exercises

When you're trying something new and you're not yet an expert, always get a second opinion and trust *that opinion*. Budgeting and sticking to a budget is important especially with flips. Remember that this house is not for *you* to live in—it's for someone else. Learn to delegate and pay people to do what they're experts at. As successful and driven as I was during this time, in hindsight, I valued my failure the most—even more than my early successes! Those mistakes were expensive at the time, but they helped me to become even better at achieving my goals, because I knew what *not* to do. I encourage you to look at mistakes and missteps as valuable detours on your journey to success. They are valuable education.

You don't have to be an expert in *all* fields—in fact, it's likely a waste of your time to learn how to be a mechanic when your goals are to build a party planning empire. You've certainly heard the phrase, "there's no 'I' in team," so do what you're good at and figure out the fastest way to get to the finish line—whether it's hiring someone, bartering a trade for skills or negotiating a trade of expertise. Beyond just supporting your success, valuing another person's expertise is also lifting their business—you are now cultivating a community of success. There is enough success going around for everyone to have some. You're only competing with yourself on your financial wellness and wealth-building journey, and seeking out others and incorporating their expertise is the fastest way to success.

1. What are your areas of expertise? Make a chart with two columns: on one side list your strengths, and on the other side, list your challenges.
2. The second column on your list is where you can delegate, trust someone else's expertise or invest in your business by investing in someone else's skills and success. Where can you create a win/win situation with that person so that you're both moving towards your goals?
3. Look at your budget and your streams of income. What "nice thing" can you afford, while still contributing to your savings and growing your business?
4. What are the most stressful pain-points in your life? Are you reacting to them, or are you accepting them?
5. Where in your life can you expand your serenity and modify your emotional responses? In reviewing the most stressful areas of your business building, who do you know who can relieve some of that stress by soliciting them for help?
6. Always reflect on the pros and cons *before and after* every investment. By weighing the risks beforehand, you'll have a clearer idea of the types of pitfalls you might encounter, and alternatively after you invest, this review will give you clarity

about the lessons you learned. What did you miss? The goal is to increase your awareness around the outcome of the choices you're making so that you are learning and growing from each experience.

For further prompts and reflections, please purchase and follow along in The Buying Time Workbook.

Chapter Seven
MONEY ON YOUR MIND...BUT WHAT'S YOUR MINDSET?

"One day, this will all be worth it." That was my mindset throughout all my business-building years. All those years of working multiple jobs and going to school while raising my kids, I saw the results of my efforts in the form of financial success—growing savings accounts, an ever-expanding real estate portfolio and a successful staffing agency that was increasing in value every year. I was seeing the proof of my delayed gratification and discipline paying off. My strategies were working, and I encourage you to embrace this philosophy in your early years—always be the hardest worker in the room.

When you're young and looking ahead, it's hard to imagine what your life might be like 10, 20 or 30 years down the line. I had a lot of responsibilities starting at 19; you may not. If you're in a position of not having children or a family to provide for, take advantage of that freedom and build, build, build! Set a goal, meet that goal and then exceed that goal. Keep your goals on your mind with every single decision you make—whether in the drive-through to pick up coffee or at the grocery store. At dinner, you can spend $8-10 on a McDonald's meal, or you can spend $5 on ground beef and $2 on a package of hamburger buns, which will give you at least four meals.

Don't know how to cook? Have you checked out the recipes and cooking tutorials on YouTube? They're free! You can learn how to make the world's best hamburger from the world's best chefs in five minutes and call it business-building. This is just an example of how your daily choices and sacrifices are investments. Choosing to eat four meals at about $2 per meal versus one meal at $8 means you can put the difference into your savings, which is smart business building.

These strategies are important, and the budget and money are important. But the engine driving the car towards your goal is your mindset. Your goals and your values are what help you form your mindset, and your mindset is what determines how you feel as you achieve success. With the ups and downs of life and business, your mindset is what will sustain your ability to always learn and move forward.

Fixed and Growth Mindsets

In the world of mindset coaching, there is a popular philosophy developed by an American psychologist named Carol S. Dweck. Her pioneering ideas explained that the way you think determines your life path. In short, she wrote that there are two types of mindset: fixed mindset and growth mindset, and these are typically learned early in life from our parents, teachers or other adults in our community or environment.

A "fixed" mindset is one that doesn't evolve with the circumstances of life. People who believe that their personality, habits and beliefs cannot be changed remain locked into doing things one way—their way. A fixed mindset believes that our intelligence and abilities cannot change or improve over time, regardless of effort. Someone with a fixed mindset avoids anything challenging, ignores advice and feedback and feels threatened when someone else succeeds or has more than they have.

On the other side of the coin, a person with a "growth" mindset knows that effort and hard work go into building skills and becoming successful. This open-minded person learns readily from others and their successes and looks for opportunities to develop themselves based on feedback from others. Every failure is a learning experience to build upon for people with growth mindsets. The most important tool in these early days of business-building is a growth mindset.

My mentor and friend Dave Austin told me this story about his abundance mindset:

> Six years ago, when we came to the doorstep of this house, fear hit. In my mind, I went, "Oh, my God, who am I to deserve this?" All of us have some part of us that thinks, "I'm not worthy." I've been on similar doorsteps for some really great things, and there have been times I've not allowed myself to walk through the door. But I walked through the doorstep to this house, looked at the realtor and said, "Don't show me another house. I don't know how I'm going to do it, but this is where we're going to live." And after making that claim, I then had to figure it out. I thought, "Okay, what are my assets?" Now, monetarily speaking, I knew I didn't have the financial assets to buy this property. But what came back to me in that quiet moment was the idea that your mind is your biggest asset. You know how to figure things out. Well, it took a while, but we've lived here for six years now. We figured it out and developed a sense of confidence by doing so.

My number one guiding principle is, "It's done unto you as you believe," and I like to say we believed our home into existence. I also firmly believe there is a spiritual connection I have that gives me an advantage, and it's because of that connection with God and feeling that presence that gives me confidence and allows me to do things that some people just can't seem to do.

Look at Henry David Thoreau, who took two years, two months and two days living near Walden Pond in a single room cabin to simply experience nature. He then wrote his book Walden, *which I regularly use in my coaching. In it, he wrote, "If one advances confidently in the direction of his dreams, and endeavors to live the life which he has imagined, he will meet with unexpected success in common hours." Now remember, courage is not the absence of fear. It's how we move through fear. Thoreau goes on to say that if you're willing to go through the invisible barrier, on the other side, new universal laws become available to you. I've lived this myself, and I believe in it thoroughly.*

What happens next is more opportunities become available to you. More answers come. I don't have to know the "how," I simply have to have the courage to move forward and the "how" just happens. Martin Luther King said, "Faith is taking the first step even when you don't see the whole staircase." Every step gives you greater vision. That's what faith is all about for me: taking that first step without knowing the how.

And so, with faith, no matter what I attempt, even if it might be challenging, I have a choice. I can take it on

with anxiety and stress, or I can take it on with enthusi-
asm, remembering we all have a choice. I choose to take
it on with enthusiasm, because I am able to deal with the
challenges better that way. Then, I trust enough that if it
doesn't work out, my wife and I have a saying for this, it
will be "this or something better." I thoroughly believe
that even if you have a little bit of a disappointment,
something better will come out of these challenges. It
might look different than you thought, but it's always
better.

I'll use a sports analogy here, because I've had so much
experience with world-class athletes and work with
some of the best in the world. They get millions of
dollars for what they do, but sometimes their value
systems get messed up. As a former professional athlete
myself, I understand this all too well.

Let's say you're a little league baseball player and you're
the best on the team. Everyone wants to be your friend,
even the parents. So, as a kid, you're popular because of
how good you are as an athlete. You grow up in that
mentality, and it remains with you as you go all the way
up and into the major leagues. Your whole value system
is based upon how well you do within your sport. You
feel valued based on your success as an athlete.

Now, here I am working with a world-class, star athlete
who is making millions of dollars, but all he wants is to
quit life. People don't know that he's miserable, but he
feels like his life is horrible. It's because his value system
is all based upon his results. And I had the same issue. I
had the same way of thinking, "I'm not enough." The

reason I felt not enough is because I was a professional tennis player, but I wasn't one of the top players in the world. In my mind's eye, I was a freaking failure. My value system was off. I based my value on my results rather than who I was as a person. When you finally shift into who you truly are and live in that and honor that, things can change overnight.

Fear doesn't throw me off anymore. I embrace the fear, and I use the fear to shift into a higher sense of focus in the right way. Fear used to distract me and get in my way. I think that when I lived in fear, I was not as successful. And it's the same with worry. Worry is good for one thing and one thing only: promoting more worry. I have learned that I attract what I fear or what I worry about. So now, when I start to worry, I take a deep breath and decide that I'm not going to go into worry-mode, because I don't want to attract more of that into my life.

My Wealth-Building Strategy

Let's talk about goals. Most of my life, my goals were about building my business and making more money. Those types of goals are definitely important. They will keep you focused, on track and moving towards lasting success. But goals are about more than dollar signs and growing bank accounts.

One thing that I wish I had done differently early on was to do some real soul searching to develop clarity on what my values are. What is the *most important* thing to me? Surely family is my top priority. After all, what else was I working for and towards if it isn't to support my family for generations to come? So that means that legacy is also one of my values: that I leave a lasting foundation for my children and their children, so that they may have it a bit easier than I did when I was growing up.

Having said that, I don't believe in free rides. Even though my children have more or less grown up with "means" because of my hard work, they have never been given everything they want. Even though I was raised in a home where my parents went into debt to give us kids whatever we wanted, I saw the pain that came as a result of that. Because I have a *growth mindset,* I knew that I could learn from my parent's mistakes and do things differently in my life. I was eager to learn from successful people who were building a legacy of generational wealth. That's what I wanted, so I knew I had a lot to learn.

On my wealth-building journey, my values were formed early in my parenting life. I decided I wanted to raise my kids to have financial hygiene and habits that I never learned growing up. If my kids don't learn from me and what I've learned, then I have really not changed anything generationally! I wanted my kids to grow up feeling confident and secure financially instead of afraid. Financial fear is insecurity.

We have a family budget, and anything my kids want that doesn't fit inside that budget needs to be negotiated and planned. They got used to me saying to them, "that's not in our budget today. We can plan for it in the future, but not today." I was teaching the importance of delayed gratification. I'll go more into how to budget family needs later.

In addition to awareness around my values, I wish I had understood the value of bigger concepts like mindset and impact. I am not an island. None of us are! We are all part of the same world and have access to the same information. Certainly, some of us start out life with certain things being a little easier, but we should never take those things for granted. Whatever kind of financial environment we grow up in, our goal should be of service to others—with our wisdom, experience, advice (when asked for!) and the fruit of our success.

As we develop wealth and see our success, a *growth mindset* involves helping other people to also grow and succeed. Certainly our immediate family and loved ones will benefit from our success, but what about our impact on our community? The world?

I have learned that how I present myself to the world is crucial. I'm not talking about flaunting my wealth and success, showing off labels and displays of the price tags on everything I own. I'm talking about how other people perceive me. I want to be approachable. I want to be open to learning from others. I want to be inspiring, loving and generous. If I am embodying these qualities, then *all of my goals align with my values, and this mindset becomes my success.*

Let's say that my target is to purchase another four properties within six months. How can I make those professional moves while also inspiring others and infusing my actions with being inspiring, loving and generous? Can I mentor someone? Can I offer a class to others so that they too can build wealth? Can I give an hour of my time and a coffee to someone who is just starting out? How do I treat my employees? Are they inspired by me? What would be the result of me providing lunch to my employees once a week?

I want to work towards and achieve my goals while being loving to individuals, my community, colleagues and the world. I must be certain that I act first with integrity. In every interaction—whether with a bank teller, someone bringing me a certificate of occupancy or the barista handing me my latte—people deserve respect. I want them to feel love radiating off of me. I want their day to be better after interacting with me than it was before.

These qualities may not sound like they have anything to

do with wealth-building. But I am writing this book because I have learned that my goals are achieved *while* I am being generous. Some may feel that it's easy to be generous when you have a lot of money in the bank. But at its core, generosity is not about sharing money—it *is* about sharing wealth—and real, unwavering wealth is about more than money.

I have abundance in my life. I am wealthy with loved ones —my children and extended family, friends and beloved colleagues who have been with me from my early days. I work with coaches and trainers who help me to be my best. These relationships are my wealth. One way I can share my wealth is to be generous with my knowledge and experience. This book is another way for me to connect with many new people, including you, who are helping me to achieve my goals while I help you achieve yours! This only works if my values drive the arrow towards the target.

Now I'll tell you my key wealth-building strategies: setting goals, hitting them and doubling them for constant growth. I apply these strategies to every type of business I do. But I don't do them without a daily commitment to be inspiring, loving and generous. When they are combined, my success is multiplied.

Tax Planning 101

I'm not a tax expert. Sure, I learned a lot when I was working for H&R Block, so when I started building wealth, I had a pretty good grasp on what to expect every year come tax time. But as my wealth grew, my expertise shrank. So the lesson here is to hire an expert!

The most important player on your team is going to be a CPA. I meet with mine every year in October to plan for the following year. During this meeting, we review potential deductions I can make, as well as any changes in tax laws and what amount of income I need to claim in order to qualify for investments and mortgages. Many self-employed people write off all their income to avoid taxes–then they can't qualify to buy rentals because on paper, they don't make enough income. If you're working with a CPA, you'll learn that when you make under $100,000 per year, the right CPA for you is very different from the CPA you'll be working with when you earn six figures, and then different again when you're earning seven. Your quality of professional will need to grow as your wealth grows to ensure you are getting the most knowledgeable person to partner with.

Working with a competent CPA, you can determine the right type of business to set up—likely an LLC or an S-corp. It's important you get expert advice before making this decision based on the type of business you are establishing.

An LLC (or Limited Liability Company) is a type of business structure that provides personal liability protection to its owner. This means that the owner of an LLC is not personally responsible for the company's debts or liabilities. LLCs do not pay taxes on their profits directly; instead their profits and losses are passed through to member(s) who report them on their individual tax returns. An LLC is typically a more flexible business type than a corporation, and it also provides more protection for investors.

An S-corporation, or S-corp, is a type of business that is taxed differently than a regular corporation. S-corps are considered pass-through entities, meaning that the company's profits and losses are passed through to the shareholders, who then report them on their individual tax returns. This allows the S-corps to avoid double taxation on corporate income. To qualify for an S-corp, you must meet certain requirements—such as having no more than 100 shareholders.

Both of these business types offer personal liability protection to owners, but they differ in terms of taxation and ownership requirements. LLCs are usually easier to form and have fewer ownership restrictions.

Job Versus Legacy

My wealth- and business-building journey has had a pretty straight path. I went to college to study business administration, which meant I could become successful in any business venture. I went to graduate school for accounting, which is an expertise that is also compatible with any kind of business. Working at the staffing agency, I saw quickly that I could get experience and expertise in that industry and then build my own business directly using that knowledge. I was excited to begin investing in real estate, and over time, I learned strategies from experts and lessons from my own experiences. But my path is not necessarily for everyone.

It doesn't matter what someone else's journey is; you must build your own path. But that doesn't mean that you are alone. There are experts and mentors in virtually every field, from app development to becoming a barber. Just remember that you must not only be an entrepreneur (a business owner), but also an innovator—find a way to do what others have done but *become better than anyone else at what you are doing and work harder than anyone else in the room.* But remember: before you start your journey, you need to establish your values.

Let's use the example above of a barber. There are many paths towards success, but let's start with a series of specific goals. The first is likely learning how to cut hair! But what kind of business owner do you want to be? Do you want to develop your community? To provide jobs and training to others? To inspire young people to see the world outside their window, street, town, city, state or country? To be generous with your time and expertise? Whatever rings true for you, you need to commit to those values and let them guide you in every decision you make.

Ask yourself, "is this step moving me closer to my business and value goals, or will I be compromising?" And being a barber is a job. How can you turn this idea into a legacy?

Some people go to school to learn—this is a good path, but it costs money. This is where a budget comes in: you figure out your tuition, you figure out how much you have to earn to pay for tuition and your rent, food, car payments, gas and household utilities.

Whether you decide school or on-the-job-training is the right path, you need to find the right kind of work—you can sweep hair at a salon or barber shop, you can work in a beauty supply store. You can start cutting hair on kids at a reduced rate, practicing all that you're learning while in school. You can work at a spa, learning about hospitality and other types of services. You can work at a makeup counter, learning about the beauty industry and the various trends and needs of different types of clientele. You can also work in any other kind of retail or service-oriented establishment and learn about customer service.

When it comes to finding the right *kind* of job, always try to keep it in line with your goals. If becoming a barber is your first goal, maybe you need to think bigger. Maybe you could own your own barber shop! In what nearby community is the most successful barber shop or salon? Who can you talk to about the challenges of being a barber shop owner? Where can you learn about starting this kind of business—finding a retail space, the expenses of buying the supplies for the shop and building a clientele? Now if you look at the business-owning model, you can learn a lot about successful business-building from other business owners, namely how to budget and how to hire staff.

How can you become an expert on all types and textures of hair? You may have to travel outside your community and visit an affluent beauty salon as well as a rural barber shop. You need to understand how elderly clients may prefer certain styles and teenagers like others. You have to learn about every texture of hair. You can find a mentor in all of these salons who are willing to teach you everything they know in exchange for sweeping hair. Or a business owner who is so impressed by how hard you work for her that she promotes you over and over. In addition to learning all that there is to learn from the community resources available to you, now turn to online tutorials. Post an ad in your area looking for "hair models" who want a free haircut that allows you to try new styles.

How often are you buying fashion magazines to learn about new trends and styles? What do the celebrities prefer? Your clientele will likely bring in a picture of their famous star and say, "I want this hair." But further, look at the photo credits: who is credited with styling the model or star's hair? Now research them and find their social media contact, because they're at the top of their game. Reach out to them and ask them for advice! Ask them how they achieved that level of success. If you reach out to 10 hair stylists, you might only hear back from one, but that person has invaluable information for you. Sometimes very successful stylists have an agent, and that agency is listed in their contact info in their bio. This is great, because now you can reach out to an agency and ask for guidance. You are likely not ready to be signed at this stage of the game, but many professionals aren't afraid to answer three questions if they have the time:

1. "My goal is to...what do you recommend to someone like me?"
2. "I like how your client...is this a path that works for most people?"
3. "What do you look for in a client?" Then, ask them if you can stay in touch and keep them informed on your progress.

Maybe owning your own business means renting a space from someone else, a landlord. But what if you owned your building outright? You now have to learn about commercial real estate. And after owning one barber shop, what if you want to open a chain of barber shops? How are you going to build and market your business?

Imagine growing your business so large that you have multiple barber shops serving multiple communities. You have other stylists working for you. You've reached such a level of success that you've opened your own school! Finally, you've even launched a successful online tutorial page where you share your industry secrets for people who subscribe to your channel, and you make advertising dollars for every view. In this scenario, you haven't just built a business; you've infused your business with your growth mindset and the values you established early on. In other words, as you were building your own success and legacy, you were also helping others to do the same thing.

This business-building model works for virtually every industry–it really just takes very creative thinking and an open mind. Every entrepreneur starts somewhere, and the most successful ones have diversified their income streams by becoming experts in every aspect of their business. The dream of becoming a barber is a small one. The dream of becoming a hair expert with a chain of stores in storefronts that they own—

a commercial real estate investor—whose businesses strengthen their communities, and the owner of an educational institution in person and on-line? That's a legacy!

Here's another example. Maybe you love music, but you're not a great musician. You do love to create playlists for friends and family, and before you know it, everyone is asking you to create a playlist for their party. It's something you love doing, but it's time consuming because you have to understand the type of party, the genres that the hosts like, the age of the attendees and how long they want music to play. You decide that you need to start charging for the personalized playlists! You're making a little money, but how can you turn this hobby into a legacy?

First, you decide what your values are and how they contribute to your vision. The reason you started creating playlists was because music brings you joy and you like to share that joy with others. Maybe you decide that your value is to spread joy through music. You vow to throw a free community block party every year to give back.

You realize that what you're basically doing is DJing. So now the research begins. Who are the highest-paid DJs in the world? How did they start? Do you want to be at the party, playing the music you've selected live? Then you need to start saving for equipment. You need to research the different vendors in your community who hire DJs for parties, weddings and bar mitzvahs. You need to get invited to all the parties you can so you can learn about what guests prefer and expect. You can also talk to the DJs at those parties. Stay after the party and offer to help them pack up their equipment in exchange for some information.

Now you're starting to really develop a vision for a career. A professional DJ! But do you want to work freelance? Is that going to be enough money to live on? What about those wedding planners and vendors—maybe they need more staff! You are now learning on-the-job all about owning a business that provides a service to the community. Catering, decor, florists, venues, valets, wait staff—all of these are aspects of event planning that you will learn about as you *work harder than anyone else and learn about everyone's job.*

Now, not only are you learning about all aspects of event planning, you're also learning what makes a great DJ. You're starting to book gigs as a DJ, and soon you're at the top of the list for all event planning businesses in the area. You're too busy! You're turning down jobs! So now it's time to start your own business training other DJs to work at events. You already have relationships with all the local vendors, and they trust you, your experience and your expertise. So they know they can also trust any staff that you've trained. And what's more, you're spreading joy to every person your music reaches.

But now is the time to really double down on your goals. You're not only going to hire and train two more DJs in the next six months, you're also going to start your own event planning business. You love seeing the joy on the faces of the wedding party and the little girl at her quinceañera, and you know what it takes for everything to come together to make a successful event. You're known in the community, you've developed relationships with every type of vendor, and you're an expert on every type of party and every type of customer. All this time, you've been throwing free parties—first a potluck on the block, now a catered festival in the park free for everyone—with donated services from all the local vendors who also benefit from community outreach and brand recognition. *That's* a legacy.

Finding Mentors Everywhere

Mentors are people who work with others to share their knowledge and expertise. They are an advisor, a teacher and coach who wants others to succeed as they have in their field of expertise. A very good mentor also wants their mentee to *exceed* their level of success.

Depending on where you are in your business-building, a mentor may be a boss, a community member or someone whom you pay to help you overcome personal or professional hurdles and challenges and move up to the next level of success.

Your first mentor might be a teacher. If you're someone with a passion for something at a young age, you can develop your skills by finding a teacher who believes in you and is willing to advise you. I want to mention that if you are a young person, always involve a parent or guardian in this relationship so that you have that extra protection from someone who may be misleading or not as trustworthy as you may have at first thought.

Whether your passion and skills are math, music, writing or acting, there is a teacher at your school or in your community who will work with you to become the best you can be and to understand your industry of interest. A good teacher and mentor will help connect you with resources and opportunities that you may not already know about, and also help you prepare for those opportunities. A competition, scholarship or program typically requires a submission process, and learning all you can from your mentor increases your chances of winning or succeeding.

If you don't have a teacher at school, there is likely someone in your community who can coach you to help you become your best. Math tutors, voice teachers, community theaters and local authors are all great resources. These mentors often charge for their services, and if you aren't in a position to pay them (or your family doesn't have the means), they may be open to a barter or internship relationship wherein you offer to correct papers, organize sheet music, plan or organize student recitals or work as an usher in exchange for their expertise. Always look for individuals who have what you want. Know when you've learned everything they have to teach you and when it's time to move on.

As you develop your skills or join the workforce, a boss or executive at the company you work for may be a great mentor. Always look for someone who has what you want—whether it's the title or knowledge—your job is to show your eagerness to become the best. You want to find someone who is in the position you want to be in—whether that is a title or a business owner. Think of it this way: you want to hire a personal trainer who is in great shape, a writer who is published or a real estate investor who owns at least 100 properties.

Once you've started your own business, you'll likely need to start paying mentors for their services. Maybe it's an accountant, a tax attorney, real estate developer or CEO. I have worked with financial advisors, CPAs and real estate coaches. I have even "leveled up" in each of these relationships, because as I achieved new levels of success, I needed to work with experts who were operating on a higher level of expertise.

If you show you're willing to invest in experts, they'll have no problem investing their time in you. I have paid many mentors over the years—experts, coaches and trainers. I always find someone who has what I want and is the best of the best.

Be the Hardest Working Person in the Room

You get out of every opportunity what you put into it. I looked at every job I ever had as an opportunity. I made myself known around every office. I was always asking questions, learning about other people's jobs and how each department contributed to the functioning of the company and the company's success. I prided myself on always following directions, always being disciplined, taking action whenever and wherever I could, being assertive and efficient with my time and others'. These qualities made me a stand-out employee, and my bosses always knew they could count on me to be a problem solver and available to help with any task in the office. They also trusted that I knew what I was doing.

By becoming an expert at everyone else's job, I made myself indispensable. But I was also building a foundation of knowledge that would serve me in my own business-building later on. This is also why it's helpful to find a job that is in line with your goals. All the effort and time you put into learning every role and how the company functions as a whole become part of your future success.

Even if the job you find isn't totally in-line with your goals, you can still benefit from being the hardest working person in the room. If your dream is to be a fashion designer, any retail job you can find can ultimately contribute to your success. You can learn about customer needs, different types of customers, fitting different body types, how to maximize profits, how to upsell customers and how to arrange a store so that the garments are most appealing. You may be in the stock room making sure the khaki pants are organized, but you can also express an interest in learning how to open the store, balance the cash register at the end of the day, manage staff and the way your store is different from other stores in the chain. You can visit those other stores and chat with other employees about their specific challenges and the sales patterns in their area.

You can learn about what people are buying from season to season, and about trends. You can learn about how managers determine purchasing decisions. Before you know it, your days working in the stockroom at a retail chain store have given you all the experience and information you need to open your own store, and how to expand that store to a national chain. The combination of having a growth mindset, making everyone's business your business and being the hardest worker in the room is the foundation for a successful future.

The Myth of the 401(k)

We've all been told that we've got the golden ticket if we get a great job working for a company that contributes to our 401(k). But what exactly is a 401(k), and is it actually important?

A 401(k) is a type of retirement savings plan that is offered by many employers. It allows you to save a portion of your income before taxes are taken out and invest that money in various funds that you can choose from. Some employers may also match some or all of your contributions, which means they will add extra money to your account based on how much you save.

A 401(k) plan has several benefits, such as reducing your taxable income, growing your savings (tax-deferred) and receiving free money from your employer. However, there are also some drawbacks, such as limited investment options, fees and penalties for early withdrawals and required minimum distributions after the age of 72. These strict rules and penalties for accessing your money before retirement can be costly—unless you qualify for an exception, such as hardship, disability or death, you will have to pay sometimes a 10 percent penalty as well as income taxes on the *total amount* if you withdraw your money early.

Some argue that 401(k)s aren't valuable because you are investing a fixed amount of money at regular intervals regardless of the market conditions, which means you may end up "buying high and selling low," and missing out on other higher-yield opportunities. 401(k)s are also not beneficial for everyone depending on your income level, tax bracket and retirement goals. If you expect to have a higher income or tax rate in retirement than when you are working, you may be better off saving in a Roth IRA or a table account instead of a traditional 401(k) or investing in real estate. If you have other sources of income in retirement, such as Social Security, pensions or annuities (a contract that requires a regular pay-out for more than one year), you may not need to save as much in a 401(k), so that money can be better invested elsewhere.

401(k)s also have high fees and expenses that can eat away at your returns, including administrative fees, record-keeping fees, investment management fees and fund expense ratios. Some of these fees may be hidden or hard to find, and can vary widely depending on your plan and your investment choices.

Many people put money into their 401(k) investment and have little to nothing invested at the time of retirement, making it low-reward passive investing. I am a firm believer that you should only put into your 401(k) what you can to max out your company match, and everything else should be put towards creating passive, sustainable income—like rental properties.

Think of rental properties as your new retirement plan. You won't have to go broke today in order to retire one day. The more passive streams of income you create now, the less you will even need a 401(k) later in life.

Your Money Belongs to Your Business

However many streams of income you have, or businesses, you need to operate each business separately. This can get difficult when you are tight on cash, but it's important that when you have extra money in a business, you leave it there and have a separate cushion for each entity. Don't take money out of your business; instead, reinvest that profit into new profit streams.

You should also be sure that each of your entities (or streams of income, or businesses) has money separated into various savings accounts for taxes, so that as you pay quarterly, you already have the money and don't have to scramble to find it. The *last* people you want to owe money to are the IRS or the state!

Multiple Budget and Income Streams

As you build up multiple streams of income, it is important that you pay yourself according to each business's budget and not overextend any one company. The other important thing to remember is to not commingle funds or profits from one business to another. Keep your budget streams separated into their respective areas of income, each aligning with the company that is the source of that money. For example, my real estate company is one stream of income and a separate business from my staffing agency. I always treated each of these companies as separate entities and didn't combine their profits, savings or debts.

Having separate accounts for your business income streams can improve your credibility and reputation with your clients, suppliers, partners and investors if you have them. It can also help you avoid mixing various business expenses which can cause confusion and errors. It also makes it easier to track and report your business income and expenses for tax purposes when they're kept separate. You can take advantage of tax deductions and credits that are available for each type of business that are unique to that market, such as writing off equipment, travel and advertising.

Chapter Seven Insight Exercises

Delayed gratification is great, but once you have abundance, you'll generate even *more* success if you have the values of generosity and find joy in helping others. Once you have some success, use your money to take people (staff, loved ones) on experiences, encourage others to save their money and stick to their budgets. Find value in helping others to follow the same plan.

1. Where can you find ways to help other people by using your skills, your money, your time or whatever you have to offer? Your specialty is your biggest asset, so use it to help others and lift them up.

2. How are you generous? Are you living in the lens of lack or do you believe there is enough for everyone?

3. How does it feel to be generous and to be a beacon of abundance for others?

4. Make a pie chart of your priorities, incorporating time, money and personal relationships, with an estimate on how much time in the day is dedicated to each. Which areas feel like you're lacking in time commitment? How can you change that? To create more time for one category, where can you delegate? Can you hire someone or trade skills to free up your time? As an example, I hired a house cleaner to lift some burden so I could spend more time with my kids. Another great hire for me was a meal service, so that instead of shopping, planning and cooking, I was spending quality time with my family. If you feel most challenged under the

"money" category, how can you change your spending habits so that you can stay on budget and invest so that you have excess money to pay off your debt sooner?

5. Instead of thinking of purchases in terms of "can I afford this and still move towards my goals?" think of certain things as priorities. If you are choosing to eat your meals out, then you are prioritizing that over your investments. You'll return to this list over and over and revise it as you feel the thrill of accomplishing goal after goal.

6. Look at your personal relationships. How much time and effort are you contributing to cultivating and building up those bonds? Where can you do better? Remember that the overall goal is balance between working (or earning), time and building valuable relationships.

For further prompts and reflections, please purchase and follow along in The Buying Time Workbook.

Chapter Eight
VALUES REVISITED AND MASTERING YOUR MINDSET

By now, you have determined what your values are and how to combine those with your growth mindset to help you achieve your goals. You have achieved some of your goals, you've doubled down and your business is growing. But I have some news that may disrupt your flow: values change. This is also part of a growth mindset.

When I first started my own business, my values were... shaky. I knew I wanted to be free from financial fear. I knew I wanted to build lasting, generational wealth so that my kids wouldn't be afraid and would learn good financial hygiene. I knew I needed to be the hardest working person in the room and that I needed to make everyone else's business my business. But those weren't values. I had success, but I was overly busy. I didn't take vacations, and I delayed more than just gratification —I was delaying joy.

In 2016, I was 29 years old with three kids and a husband who was struggling. Yes, it's true: you can have a lot of money and success, and you can still struggle. I had a moment of clarity, and saw that my husband was really and truly suffering from PTSD that had been getting progressively worse. If I was to be able to help him at all, and to be present and available for my family, I not only had to look closely at my values, I had to completely change my mindset. It was time to build something even more valuable than my business.

One thing I learned during this time is the value of putting the oxygen mask on yourself first—you can't truly be of service to others or be helpful if you yourself are not well. I couldn't be of service to my husband or my family if I didn't make some serious personal changes.

I looked closely at my mindset. For so many years, I had been thinking: *Build! Grow! MORE!* I found myself on a treadmill of thinking that what I had and who I was would never *be enough.* My self-talk—the things I thought about myself and my life—was based on a belief system that I was always lacking something. I needed to have and be more. It was time to focus on my own personal development journey and to cultivate my feelings of self-worth and how I defined happiness.

When I turned 30, I was a millionaire. What an achievement! As part of my new thinking, I started taking vacations with my family every six to eight weeks. We would visit Cabo San Lucas and Cancun, Hawaii, the Dominican Republic, Seattle–anywhere we felt excited about, we'd visit. Those vacations were wonderful bonding experiences that I will always treasure. But the toll of taking time off with my grind mindset meant that when I wasn't on vacation, I was working twelve hours a day, Monday through Sunday. And on those vacations, I was still constantly checking my phone and responding to emails. I rarely actually took time off to be present with my family and to really be in my life and the moment. Eventually, I hired a mental coach.

The Difficult Work of Changing Your Mindset

Dave Austin was someone who could help me, one-on-one, change my mindset and develop a better attitude that would help me transform my life. I learned that I could only be so successful with my old ideas of success. I began to understand that I wanted to be successful *and* fulfilled. I learned that these are two different things! I saw quickly that my self-worth was tied to the money I was earning and the financial and professional goals I was achieving. I had to shift my focus and my attitude. My oxygen mask was believing that *I am enough as I am.*

Because Dave has had such a long and interesting journey with money and his value system, I asked him about when his own shift happened:

> *Again, my dad was a Navy chaplain, so that meant we were brought up in a very traditional Christian home. The values I learned revolved around faith, honesty and truthfulness. Your word is your word. Stand up for who you are. In WWII, my dad led the charge at Iwo Jima without a weapon. And about 50 percent of those on that first wave of soldiers hitting the beach were killed. Since he was out in front, some people ask my dad, "Why would you lead the charge? You didn't have to do that." And he would always say, "That's where I was needed most. I love God, and I love my Marines." That really stuck with me: Where am I needed most in life? I ask that question all the time.*
>
> *My dad was brave enough to take on machine gun fire for what he believed in, but there have been times in my life where I've asked myself, "Am I brave enough to take this on?" Then I realize it's not machine gun fire. I don't*

think I could do what he did, but if my dad was willing to take on machine gun fire, I can take on business failures and whatnot. I can take on someone else's words and criticism. I can go ahead and do whatever it is that scares me or makes me uncomfortable. This was a big building block for me to be willing to do the crazy impossible things I've done and continue to do.

Over the years, my relationship with God has grown stronger than ever, but I've changed in that now, I am more spiritual than religious. In what I've learned through traveling the world, reading books and coaching is that my faith is stronger than ever. It's not church every Sunday and prayer before meals and all of that. It's not so structured; it's more just a very personal relationship with God. It's individualized, with a big dose of living in gratitude first and foremost.

If I look back, I remember that I received the Presidential Merit Award from the Grammys. I had a hit record on the radio. I've been in movies and television. I've coached some of the best athletes in the world. I've written bestselling books and blah, blah, blah. But I've always felt that even with all of that, I was never enough. None of it was that amazing in my eyes. It was never enough. Then, eventually, I figured out that I was worthy—regardless of how much I made financially or how many things I had or hadn't done.

I've realized my most important value is my family: my wife and my kids come first, above everything. And I feel so blessed because of it—so blessed. At times, I still need to make tough choices like deciding whether or not to take on a business opportunity, but now I look at things differently. I don't just do it. I go to my wife first and say, "Here's an opportunity..." For example, I just came back from Egypt. I got hired to go work with a group of business leaders in Cairo. After I orchestrated my fee and everything, my wife traveled with me so we could share the experience together. We had a cruise down the Nile and did all kinds of really cool things. Now, I like to flip things around so I can fit my work life into my family experiences, instead of trying to fit my family into my work life.

Learning to Lean Into Abundance

As I shifted my focus and changed my attitude, I saw that I was granted even *more* abundance because my definition of abundance had changed. My new mindset meant I was living more generously, helping others and living in gratitude. I was still successful—even more so than before—but my success was much, much more meaningful.

Because I was so young when I started grinding and building, I wasn't able to see that many of my choices were based on subconscious decisions—reactions based on my previous life experiences instead of who I wanted to become. I was trying to build a future based on where and who I used to be. I was trying to build a future with my past as my foundation. And my past wasn't strong enough to support how big I wanted my future to be!

Subconscious decisions are the choices we make without any real awareness around *why* we're making those decisions. Sure, life experience is valuable. If I were in a car accident because I was texting and driving, I would hope that moving forward I would understand that I will very likely have *another* car accident—maybe a worse one—if I continue to text and drive. So I make a decision to never text and drive again. That's a *conscious* decision—one that is thoughtful and informed.

I wanted to become the most authentic version of myself that I could be, which meant every choice and decision I made had to come from a place of who I wanted to become instead of based on the experiences in my past. The most valuable lesson in this mindset shift was learning how to respond to stress. I needed to stop reacting and to begin consciously choosing to respond based on the person I *want to be.*

I want to be generous. I want to be patient. I want to be free of fear about things that have happened in the past and the things that may or may not happen in the future. I want to be gracious and grateful. I want to live in such a way where I have so much gratitude for all that I have, that I see and feel my abundance and can give freely because I am confident there will *always be enough.* And I need to believe that I am enough. If I am making choices and decisions based on who I want to be, I'm moving myself and my life in the direction towards the life I want.

My growth mindset had led me here, but it was time to grow even bigger. I needed to shift my mindset to one of *abundance.* In his book, *7 Habits of Highly Effective People,* author Stephen Covey discusses the value of believing that there are enough resources, time and opportunities for everyone to achieve their goals. We are not in competition with each other, and we all have access to the universe and its abundance. An abundance mindset focuses on the positives in every scenario. We have a choice in literally every moment to either react to something based on fear, scarcity and previous negative experiences, or to consciously choose to remember all that we're grateful for. The peace that comes from that choice results in trusting that there is enough for everyone.

World-renowned entrepreneur, philanthropist and mindset guru Tony Robbins teaches that gratitude directly leads to success in all areas of life because: "When you are grateful, fear disappears and abundance appears." This makes it easy to celebrate when others succeed or win, and turns you into a generous person who gives freely and without fear.

I embraced the abundance mindset and began to help whomever I could whenever I could. Living in gratitude and generosity means I am also open to receiving whatever comes my way, and to receive it as the gift that it is. I began to live as the person I wanted to become. This internal shift turned me into someone who could easily be of service to others. When I'm in service, I receive more than I could ever imagine. The more I give, the more I get. As I evolved my thinking, the way I lived changed. My relationships changed. Everything in my life, even the inevitable challenges of life, were now gifts contributing to my abundance.

One enormous gift to come from my mindset shift was seeing time as a gift. Even if my previous mindset that was focused mostly on hustling and earning wasn't sustainable, it had gotten me all that I had today. I had two valuable businesses and enough wealth in the bank to last generations. Instead of dwelling on regrets for how I used to prioritize work over my personal connections and living in the moment, I chose to have gratitude for everything I had built and the fortitude, discipline and work ethic that helped me to build it. But it was now time to enjoy it.

Some economists have said that "time is money." I prefer to say that time is a gift. And in my case, I spent so much time building my businesses without also knowing that I was buying myself time—a valuable present that I would be opening later in life.

My mindset change meant that how I spent my time was

the most valuable type of spending I could imagine. And because I truly saw all the abundance in my life, I wanted to also experience the joy of sharing it with the people I love most.

Family became my number one priority. I began taking one-on-one trips with each of my children. I was also now modeling for them my new values of being authentic, being of service and being aware and conscious of all my choices as I began to live the life I always wanted.

I had come so far financially and even mentally, but something still wasn't clicking. I was misunderstanding the definition of balance; it's not swinging from one extreme to the other, but having both sides of the scale equally balanced. And if I was going to lean in any direction, shouldn't it be towards joy?

Here's a chart demonstrating how my values and mindset have evolved over time:

Old Values and Mindset	New Values and Mindset
Work ethic	Compassion
Generous (to a fault–often compromising myself)	Generous (with reason and purpose)
Assertive	Gratitude
Honest and ethical	Honest and ethical
Accountability	Self-accountability (no longer worrying about holding others accountable and learning that I can only control myself)
Disciplined	Disciplined
Determined	Determined
Conditional self-love (I was only worthy of loving myself if I succeeded)	Unconditional love (myself and others)

You can see these aren't *huge* shifts in my thinking, but they were big enough to change my life dramatically. I hope that you can make a similar chart by the time you're done reading this book, and then again five or 10 years from now.

Chapter Eight Insight Exercises

You know what your values are, but do you know who you want to be? Let's dive in with a little exercise to help you focus on your ideal life and the future beyond your dreams.

Mindset Quiz:

1. What are some decisions you have made that are tied to where you come from?
2. What are your fears? Write down the *worst things* that could happen.
3. Write out a dream day in the life you want to live. How do you feel?
4. Think of a stressful situation in your life—with money, relationships or work. How did you respond or react? What would the "ideal you" do differently?
5. How do you feel when someone else wins or succeeds? For example, someone you work with gets a promotion or a friend gets a new car from their parents.
6. When was the last time you did something nice for someone without expecting something in return? This should be something other than a birthday or holiday gift.
7. Where are some areas in your life that you can be generous with your time or knowledge? Do you ever volunteer your time serving others?
8. Go through your house or room and pick three to five things that would make someone else happy. Give them away!

9. Think of three things that went "wrong" in the past. Write down how they made you feel at the time. Now write down how the ideal future you—one who is confident, grateful and believes that there is enough for everyone—would respond to these challenges.

10. Write down 10 things that you are grateful for. I recommend starting each and every day with this exercise!

For further prompts and reflections, please purchase and follow along in The Buying Time Workbook.

Chapter Nine
SOMEDAY IS NOW

After all these years of being an expert in my business and everyone else's, the time had come to become an expert on the relationships in my life, being available to my family, and primarily to be of service to my husband and to help him heal. My new mindset was like a new pair of glasses through which I looked at my life and all that I had built and examined how it was impacting my life.

I became very aware of just how unhealthy some of my professional relationships were. I looked closer at the way I was communicating and where I was starting to grow in a new direction. Because I was so focused on building love and compassion in all areas of my life, toxic and unhealthy relationships and interactions started to really stand out in a bad way. In tandem with wanting to dedicate my time to focus on the relationships that mean the most to me, I also wanted to live a less rigid and structured lifestyle. I was ready for a new journey.

As I experienced these internal changes, I reached a point where I felt ready to take another leap. If I was to truly be of service to others, I needed to make myself totally available to my loved ones. I also wanted to begin sharing my success with others in a committed and meaningful way. I decided that it was time to retire, and in April of 2022, I sold my staffing agency for more money than I could have ever imagined.

Big decisions like this can be scary. But because I was making this decision with the belief that I had enough and because the decision was in line with the future I was envisioning for myself, I only felt confident that it was the right decision at the right time. All of that delayed gratification and sacrifice in my early years had brought me here, and I was ready to be a full-time wife and mother.

I was so ready to begin my new phase of life, and I began fantasizing about being of service to others, inspiring young people to build wealth like I had, which was completely in line with my desire to inspire others. The "someday" that I was delaying all my gratification for was *now*. The future was thrilling, and the opportunities were infinite.

Then, it happened.

On July 27th, 2021, my husband took his life.

Time stopped. Nothing mattered anymore.

Dealing with the Aftermath of Unexpected Tragedy

Like most people going through the stages of grieving, I looked back over my life and wondered what I could have or should have done differently.

> *I could have saved him, if only I had...*
> *It was my fault, because I failed to de-escalate the situation.*
> *It was my responsibility to fix him.*

Things could have been different if we had...
It was my fault. I should have seen the warning signs
this time.
I had talked him off the ledge before, but did it wrong
this time.
I didn't do enough to keep him alive.

I cried for two months, experiencing the grief, sorrow and guilt as a bottomless well of murky emotions. I got all the help that is so important to get when you experience trauma, are dealing with grief and need to navigate the stages of mourning. I got my children the support they needed. It was a "circle the wagons" moment where we protected ourselves and cared for each other and took stock of all the pieces of our lives that we had left. We were bereft. We were heartbroken. I was in despair for myself and my children.

Even with all the help we were getting, I worried about their emotional and spiritual states. But the one thing I did not do was worry about money. I opened the gift that I had bought myself over my years of wealth-building: time.

I had bought myself time to grieve, for as long as it took.
I had bought myself time to work with mental health
professionals, to really understand the grieving process.
I had bought myself time to spend with my children
when they needed me most.
I had bought myself time not worrying about how we
would pay for funeral expenses.
I had bought myself time not worrying about mortgage
payments or a reduction in household income.
I had bought myself time to look closely at the life I had
built, and to value and cherish it.
I had bought myself time free from worrying about how

long paid leave would last, and when I would be
expected to return to the office.
I had bought myself precious time, free from financial
fear.

The Life-Saving Power of Buying Time

As I worked through all of my pain, I remembered the value of
the abundance mindset. I suddenly felt deep and profound
gratitude that I had started evolving my financial philosophy
and value system when I did–otherwise I would never be able
to see that there was light in every darkness. Even after devas-
tating loss, all my efforts in the previous years—the building of
my businesses and wealth, my years of hard work—weren't for
nothing. They were all part of the bedrock of resilience that
was getting me through this darkness.

Two of my dearest friends who were holding my hand
through the mourning process helped me to reframe my feelings of guilt. I truly believed that my husband would be alive if
only I had done better—worked harder and done a better job at
de-escalating his extreme moods. My friends helped me to see
that I was dwelling on the negative story. That even though
there is nothing positive about losing someone you love, I had
actually kept my husband alive five years longer than he would
have been without my support. That was five years with him
that I and my children benefited from because I had truly done
my best, and it was enough. I was enough. I began to think of
those five years as a victory.

The same friends also convinced me to attend a Tony
Robbins event called Date With Destiny. I had of course heard
of Tony Robbins and knew he was a powerhouse of wisdom
and positivity. How could I say no?

This event changed me in a profound way. I already

believed much of what Tony teaches, but what I learned that day was that I needed to look at my life through a lens of love, not lack. I learned how to change my story. The story I kept playing over and over in my head was that I didn't have enough, and that if I stopped working twelve hours a day, seven days a week, that I would lose everything, including my identity. The most painful part of my story was that I had failed to keep my husband alive, and that it was my fault that he was dead. He took his life because I wasn't enough—I wasn't good enough, strong enough or smart enough. I didn't do enough. I was telling myself this story, and I was believing it.

But the thing about our stories is that we are the author. We can rewrite and change them any time we want. I learned that by changing my story, I could change my life.

I began to see all the years I spent building my life based on my old values of working harder, hitting goals, doubling goals and grinding—even though I was driven by fear, I was developing the framework and the financial freedom to grieve all these years later. My emotional survival mode shifted that day to living in gratitude; unlike most people who lose a spouse, I was not drowning in debt and uncertainty.

With my refreshed spirit and mindset of love and gratitude, I was able to be more present and available, and a beacon of light for my children. We were still grieving—and always will be—but grief feels lighter when it's buoyed by gratitude. And I also began to realize that I didn't have to give up on my dreams of becoming an inspirational leader for others—particularly young people—as they begin their paths to prosperity. I just had a new way of defining it.

My life might look different from what I planned, but the benefit of remaining open-hearted and generous with an abundance mindset means that I can take in my new circumstances and pivot; I'm still writing the book I always wanted to write, but now my message is deeper and more focused on building a healthy mindset first that will help you have a more meaningful journey, one that defines success as fulfillment, not riches.

One important part of changing our minds and mindset is to incorporate this positive messaging in our daily lives. One way is through repetition, and a tool that many coaches recommend is to write down positive affirmations where you can see them every day when you wake up. This is like the energizer before you have your coffee and start your day. Here are some exercises that will help you stay in the moment, and center your actions and decisions around your core values and personal goals.

Chapter Nine Insight Exercises

Time is not guaranteed. You should spend each and every day loving your life and living in abundance and joy. Here are some exercises to help you start each day on the right foot.

Affirmation Exercises:

1. Write yourself a letter of praise. Identify specific attributes and successes that have helped to shape your life up to now. Write this as though you are 20 years older and so proud of all that you've accomplished. Imagine you are your own parent, and write everything you wish you heard every day from someone who is *so proud* of you.

2. Make a list of attributes you want to become, and write notes that you can place around your house (or in a journal that you can look at every day) to remind you that you already embody those

qualities. *I am loving. I am inspiring. I am generous. I am loved. I am a leader. I am ready! I have everything I need. I have enough. I am enough.* Now you can go about your day with these attributes at the center of all your actions and decisions. *What would a generous person do at this coffee store? What would a loving person do for their fellow students? What would an inspiring person do in the breakroom at work?*

3. What is your definition of success? Mine is feeling fulfilled–always feeling like I have more than enough and that I am enough. Maybe for you it's about making the time every day to be of service to others as a reminder that you have enough. Maybe it's happy children who have all that they need. Maybe you feel successful when you have accomplished a full day of work and still have time to take a walk on the beach to see the sunset. Write down your personal definition of success, and revisit it from time to time, knowing that it may evolve over time. That's a good thing! That's a growth mindset.

4. What are some areas of abundance in your life? How can you share this abundance with others?

5. Look at your list of goals. Now rewrite them with a mindset of abundance. If your goal was to "pay off college in six months," maybe you can extend that to eight months, take a portion of that payment and donate it to an animal shelter. Remember you have enough and there is enough!

6. Revisit your list of goals regularly. Categorize them as daily goals, weekly goals, monthly, end of the year and five-year goals.

7. Who in your life is a priority? How do you share your abundance with them? Do they know how grateful you are for them? Practice sharing with the important people in your life that you're grateful for them. Taking that extra step to express your gratitude instead of just listing it out on paper is the most powerful way to build your relationships. It also builds up the people in your life, reinforcing their own affirmations.

For further prompts and reflections, please purchase and follow along in The Buying Time Workbook.

Chapter Ten
THE PRESENT

When I think back to those terrifying days in my early life when I was feeling stranded and helpless in an overheated car with my mom, I am struck by how different life can be. Yes, I was a child and there was so much out of my control, and there was a lot I didn't understand about life yet. But conversely, there is nothing more terrifying than the sudden loss of an important figure in your life—at any age—whether it's a parent, spouse or any other loved one. But little Heidi stranded on a freeway was feeling something that adult Heidi burying her husband wasn't feeling: fear.

That fear I experienced as a kid was coming from a lack of planning, a lack of preparation, a lack of communication, a lack of sound values and a lack of financial hygiene. Life comes at you fast, and my parents weren't prepared with a financial plan—and like a lot of couples starting a family, they ended up building their lives on a shaky foundation of financial insecurity. The result was a life built on lack, not abundance.

Today I have an abundance of love, health, friendships,

family, opportunities, ideas, choices and time. It's not the money I have now that makes me happy. It's not the financial security that makes me feel fearless. It's the foundation of fulfillment. The *only* thing I lack is fear.

The time since my husband took his life has not been easy. But I would argue that it has been significantly easier than it would have been without all my previous hard work and hustle, building and preparing for a future and the unknowns I might encounter. My time was an investment in those building years even more than my money was. The long-term payoff of that investment was more time.

Most people, when they lose a spouse, plummet into not only despair, but fear. All of the expenses that come with burying a loved one are a surprise, even if you *have* planned. Funerals, burials, time lost in grief and lost working hours adds a whole other layer of stress and worry. Most people don't have the time to grieve or to invest in their suddenly fractured futures by getting the mental health support they need. They are broken, broke, afraid and have little to no time to focus on what matters most: living a life of fulfillment.

Don't get the impression that this period of time was easy. I started losing money for the first time in my working life, and anxiety was trying to creep in. But because I was working with therapists and coaches, I had regular reminders that while I was missing a husband and losing money, I was also living a life of abundance. They helped me remember to stay in gratitude.

I looked for ways to continue to be generous, since that was one of my primary values. I met a woman who was in a similar situation to me, having recently and suddenly lost her husband. He was her sole provider, and she didn't know how she would pull through this period of her life. Even though I was losing money, I gave her money. I also shared her GoFundMe page with my community, many of whom are wealthy investors and business owners, to help raise money in support of her and her family during their time of grief. I had bought myself time, and I wanted to also buy her time.

Yes, I had bought myself time—and it was time I spent some of that savings. I spent it on myself and on my children. We huddled together, held each other and grieved. We got help from counselors. We got support from friends and family. We worked with coaches and experts who know about grief, PTSD and recovering from loss. Because I had nothing but time to focus on myself and my recovery, the hardest part of my grieving period was shortened—condensed in a way that was a luxury.

While I felt like my life was folding in on itself, it was actually expanding. I was growing my internal wealth to such an extent that I couldn't imagine the dividends. After months and months of work, one of my therapists gave me an exercise. He told me to practice dating, just to see what it felt like.

I hated it.

I registered for a dating app that helps women plan dates by being the initiator, which made me feel safer and a little more in control. Nearly every date I went on, the guy would raise a red flag for me—making me doubt the process. I didn't want to go on a second date with almost anyone. It seemed futile and like a waste of time.

But I was never afraid of hard work. Because I was committed to building a new future for myself, I followed my own rules and worked with the experts. I doubled down on my investment—this time, my investment was myself. I worked with both my therapist and my coach to really look deeply into what I wanted my life to look like, and I saw clearly that I didn't want to spend it alone. They helped me to outline what an ideal man would look like for me. Not his appearance, but his qualities. My mentor Dave Austin had me write out the following:

How would he respond to life situations and challenges?
What type of work does he do?
What are his values?

I even got a random message from a psychic medium who told me to "think outside the box." I was very thorough and specific with my check list, just as I would be with a business plan.

The next day, I joined a new dating website. The first man to message me was named Rob. He worked with people struggling with addiction and recovery as a life coach. He was a mental health advocate. He was a public speaker, advocating for mental health, speaking to large crowds and in schools. He was living a life of service, and got great joy helping others and being generous. He was writing a book, *Warrior in the Garden*, about being prepared for the hard things in life. He didn't just tick every single box on my list, he blew me away.

We were married in an intimate ceremony on September 10th, 2023 in a castle in Scotland.

This fairy tale ending didn't come easy—I put in the hard work! But Rob has been the missing puzzle piece for me and my kids. He fit into our lives effortlessly, as if we had been holding a place just for him. He has become a role model for my kids, showing them a clear path through their grief. He was and is the perfect person to work with to help me process my survivor's guilt.

Happiness following loss comes at a price—guilt creeps in, and it is a powerful obstacle between me and joy. I was being haunted by flashbacks, seeing my husband take his life over and over again in my mind. This trauma was replaying on repeat, blinding me from seeing any path that might make it possible for me to move forward.

How can I dare to be happy with a dead husband? What right do I have to live the rest of my life happy and free, while he lived such a painful life, leaving us so abruptly? Weren't widows supposed to be unhappy for a predetermined number of years—isn't there a formula for how long and how you're supposed to grieve?

These fears and feelings are all part of a stigma that surrounds suicide and the trauma experienced by survivors. Feelings of blame, shame, abandonment and rejection are normal for people who lose someone to suicide, because they are trying to make sense of the death and their role in it. It's also normal for survivors to feel an increased level of responsibility, like I did. A voice in their head that is constantly saying, "It's all your fault." But because I have a team of professionals, I can process my grief and all of these passing, intrusive thoughts and feelings as part of my journey. They help to shape me, but they don't define me.

Because Rob has such an evolved understanding of grief and mental wellness, he is a constant reminder that *success of any kind comes no matter what* as long as your mindset is centered on abundance and gratitude. He has helped me and my kids find our joy. We are here in this life for a finite amount of time, and we are meant to be fulfilled. Luckily, I already knew that feeling, and it was already solidified as my core value. I can confidently take steps towards a happy future—my newest goal—because I have a clear vision of what I want for my life.

This book has evolved so much since my first attempts to write it. What started out as purely a financial book has become a commitment that I share with you to have a purposeful journey with fulfillment as the master plan. Instead of just helping young people get rich, my vision is to help and inspire others to reach fulfillment at a much younger age than their peers. I want to help young people to be consciously aware of their values and mindset early, rather than waiting until they are in their 30s to start planning their future. My hope is that the tools and strategies in this book will help you build and live a beautiful life during your journey, not just once you achieve your goals or reach an ambiguous destination. It is said that "life is what happens while you're planning," but I believe that planning can help you live that life more fully.

Now, armed with a clear vision of your values and your mindset, you're ready to build. You have a foundation based on your definition of fulfillment, and it will support you as you set —then double—your financial, mental and spiritual goals.

Now, go be the hardest-working person in the room, and don't forget to be generous every step of the way.

Acknowledgments

I'd like to thank my parents and my family. While I didn't grow up with a silver spoon, I did grow up in a loving home where I know they did their best each and every day. The work ethic I learned from both of them is instilled in me and all my siblings, and I am forever grateful for their example and encouragement. My parents raised me to believe in myself and constantly praised me. I know I can do anything because *they* believed I could do anything and were always there to support me. The way my family has stepped up in my hardest times is a testament to how well my parents did at leading by example and showing how to be loving, generous and inspiring. I am inspired by each of my family members in different ways and appreciate their ongoing love and support. I'm so fortunate we are so close and that we are always there for each other.

I'd also like to thank my children.

Kaden—you came to me at a young age, and I am so incredibly grateful for our journey and our relationship. I changed my life in a dramatic way to be the best I could for you, and looking back, you are the number one reason I made it to where I am. You were my main goal and I was committed to giving you the best life. You are beyond amazing. You have all of my strengths and none of my weaknesses. You are brilliant yet balanced. You are hardworking and humble. I wouldn't change anything about you or our relationship, and I am so grateful that I have a best friend for life. I believe in you, and I know you will do amazing things in the world.

Cole—You have always been such a funny, strong-willed kid. You know what is right and what is wrong, and you aren't afraid to say it or to stand up for the right thing. You have a way with words where you can get yourself out of anything, and I genuinely believe you will make a great salesman one day. You are ethical and smart. You remind me a lot of your dad. I know he was hardest on you, and I hope you know how proud I am of your strength and ability to love through the hardest of times.

Miles—My sweet boy. You are the kindest, sweetest kid on the planet. You care so much about everyone being happy, and regardless of how people treat you, you always show respect and love. You remind me so much of my mom. You both are amazing at turning the other cheek and continuing to stay true to who you are. You are so smart and have the best communication skills. I'm in awe of your kindness and loving personality.

I'd like to thank my husband, Rob. I thank God every day for giving you to us. You are exactly what we needed and you came at just the right time. I never knew a fairy tale love like this was really possible, and I feel so grateful to experience this. I wish everyone had a love like ours, because then the world would most definitely be a better place. You are such a great example to my boys, and I appreciate your constant effort to prepare them for life and help them become good men. I'm grateful for Sophie's influence on you, and now on me and my boys. She is so sweet and kind, yet fierce and fun. Our family dynamic is so safe and healthy, and I am so grateful for that. I never knew how much my soul needed yours to be complete.

I'd like to thank Matt Atkinson. He has taught me everything I know about real estate and has guided and mentored me through plenty of complicated situations with patience and understanding. I met Matt at 19 while buying my first house and still work with him today, learning from him about navigating changes in the market. I appreciate your love and support for my success and fulfillment.

I'd like to thank Dave Austin. Thank you for your contribution to the book, but more importantly, thank you for the positive influence you have had on my life and my mindset. I grew a lot as a person with your guidance and help. I would not be the businesswoman, mother, wife or friend I am today without the years of working with you to improve. Thank you for your time and experience.

Last but not least, I'd like to thank Rick McNulty, my late husband. We met when I was a baby with a baby, trying to take over the world. You supported my dreams and helped the best you could. You constantly tried to be the best husband, father and soldier that you could be, despite your traumatic childhood and life experiences. You are still the boys' hero, and I hope that you have finally found the peace you always dreamed of. We both know I tried to give you the best life and show you what a healthy, loving family looked like. In hindsight, there are definitely things I wish I could've done differently, but at the end of the day, all I can do is apply the lessons I've learned to become the best version of myself and continue to try to make the world a better place.

We love and miss you.

About the Author

Heidi McNulty is a real estate investor, entrepreneur, speaker and widowed mother of three children. After buying her first property at 19, she scaled her real estate portfolio to more than $15 million, then sold her business for seven figures to retire at 35 (while still flipping between 12 and 20 homes a year).

McNulty is a mentor to young people, beginner real estate investors and startups as well as a frequent guest speaker at real estate investor associations in Utah, including the SLREIA and the UVREIA. In 2022, she was a guest speaker at Tony Child's Pivot Point event and a featured mentor on *America's Real Deal*.

In 2023, McNulty met and married Rob Eastman, the "tattooed life coach," and together they are launching The Village Effect, a revolutionary holistic wellness program offering counseling, family services and life and finance coaching. She lives in Utah with her family. *Buying Time* is her first book.

www.ingramcontent.com/pod-product-compliance
Lightning Source LLC
Chambersburg PA
CBHW030526210326
41597CB00013B/1038